DESIGNED TO STICK

Another practical guide to starting the business of your dreams

---

RICK JESSE

Dogtooth

Contents

Intro

Employment as we know it is changing, and more and more people are choosing "a life of choice". Choice based around where they work, how they work, what they work on, and how often they work. There was a time when people would decide on a career, find the biggest and best employer in the area, and stay with them for life. However, technology has completely changed all of that, because today, if you wished, you could be in an exotic location working on your laptop, managing your globally distributed workforce. Of course, it isn't a simple process to get to that point, but it is more than possible and people are choosing to do just that. Some people are also choosing to do what they love, this could be baking, coaching, sculpture, writing, or handcrafting quality leather goods.

People are making choices about what they exchange their energy for. So what was once seen as an obligatory 40+ hours a week labour for an employer might now be 20 hours working for yourself and 20 hours reading, socialising, or volunteering. This book is about making you aware that these choices are not as hard as you may think.

The Entrepreneur's Journey

I cannot be clearer when I say I'm still on my own journey. After twelve years, I should perhaps be further down the road to success than I am. Some of the reasons for this will be explained in the following chapters—and hopefully, you will heed them, rather than repeat them yourself. I'm not a millionaire, but I have grown my business to earn a reasonable amount of money and provide a good standard of living for my family.

However, money is only part of the plan. Ask me whether I feel fulfilled. Do I have joy in running my own business, even during hard times? You bet I do! Being the master of my own destiny is priceless. If you have a passion for something but don't know where to start, this book will be right up your street.

I can't guess exactly where you're coming from when reading this book. You could be a creative looking to freelance, or a freelancer looking to grow a business. You might be an accountant at one of the big four, dreaming about opening a motorcycle shop. Or you might be a gym lover looking to leave a paying-yet-life-sucking-black-hole-of-a-job to become a personal trainer. Or you may be in one of the zillions of other possible scenarios. You may have started your journey already, or you might be early on in the process, taking a course to confirm your skills. Maybe you have everything in place ready to roll, but are struggling to leave the security of that regular wage. But the one thing we all have in common is that we all have to start somewhere.

This book should give you a clear idea of what you need to get started, of what to expect, and how to excel at turning your dream into reality.

Who Is This Book For?

This book is for those of you who want to start something by selling a skill, product, or service. It's for those who have little investment and the need to be profitable virtually immediately. This is for real-world businesses, where you have a passion or a dream that you want to turn into a paying reality. To be a little more colourful, it's for people who are sick of working for "the man" and want to forge their own path. It is for those who don't want to see the big-hairy-beast-of-regret waiting at their deathbed.

What This Book Is About

In this book, there are lessons I learned on my journey from starting out as a freelance graphic designer in my one bedroom flat, to running a fully-fledged business with staff, selling several different products into B2B and B2C markets, and having them featured on several TV shows. Want to know how to do "a bit on the side"? Need to know how to get the money in? Want to see how systems can help? How to create a brand? Or how to make money from products if you package up your skills or services? You'll discover these things within the pages of this book.

I'll cover not only the practical work you need to put in to achieve this, but also some of the thoughts and mental processes you need to understand as an entrepreneur, such as creativity, psychology, and business ethics. We'll take a look at the things that help you achieve success and the things that hinder you. There's also a healthy dose of motivation included for those who need that final bit of encouragement.

Nothing happens without effort. So let's get started!

About the Author

Who am I and why am I writing this book? Well, it all started a long time ago, like most stories. If you're not in the mood for a story, you can skip to Chapter 1. This chapter just provides some context on how I ended up writing a book on starting the dream business.

My name is Rick Jesse. I am actually a Richard, but virtually no one knows me as that. At points in my life, I have also been called Ricky, Rich, Jess, and Jenkins. I am a graphic designer by trade. I live in a rural market town in North Yorkshire and I run a small business punching well above its weight. Our products have been featured on several TV shows and we have worked with scores of high-profile brands.

It's hard writing a book that balances personal stories and useful content. I have read plenty of books that are self-glorifying CVs. I have also read books that became boring and lacked context, leaving me wanting to know more about the author. I have Scottish and Irish blood and I like a good story. So my intention is to mix the experiences and knowledge from my business life with a few stories along the way. Like parables, a good story should have meaning and entertain.

What Made Me

When I was young, I became known as "one of those arty kids". At primary school, I loved painting and drawing, which was noticed and encouraged. It therefore became part of my identity.

As I went through secondary school and on to graphic design at college, the art thing sort of helped me, as I was never one of those lads who enjoyed football or did badass stuff. Though I did once score a "try" at my first, and only, game of rugby. In that single moment of sporting glory, I caught the ball and whilst everyone was wondering what to do next, I just ran. That turned out to be a good thing!

So, team sports and school in general were not my cup of tea. I was creative and interested in cars. So when my CDT teacher asked in class "What do you want to do?" I said, "I want to be a car designer". However, rather than being encouraged to follow my dream, what happened was what happened to many kids back in the 80s, I was told—point blank—"You'll never be a car designer!" I was crushed!

This is not a book where that put-down motivated me to go on to greatness. No, sadly that teacher crushed my dream. But with most things in life, if you are passionate enough, you can find a way.

What did you do when you looked through the careers book at 13? I looked at any job that meant I could get paid, a lot, to create stuff with my imagination. I first looked at being an Architect. I remember the careers book said earnings of up to £120k (back in 1988, money like that was lottery money). Then I read you needed to do a lot of higher education. So that was out.

The next best job I could find was Graphic Designer, a position that could earn up to £60k. Again, this was good money in the 80s, though many years later my colleagues and I would find that laughable. Becoming a designer meant I had to commit to more education. But I felt that it was my kind of thing, so the trade-off was worth it. At 13, I decided to become a graphic designer.

Fast forward six years, I got my National Diploma in Graphic Design. I went on to a Higher National Diploma course, but sadly I got kicked off that course - oops. I was a bit gutted at the time, but fortunately, within a few months, I got a job in the print industry.

Geek

Whilst I was encouraged to draw and paint at school, my second passion was computers. At school, back in the late 80s, this was a monochrome PC. At college, it was the Mac. At my first job interview ever, it went something like this: "We see you 'do computers'…would you like a job?" If only interviews were that easy these days!

Being an early adopter has its advantages. Firstly, you have skills or products that few people have, so you stand out in the marketplace. Secondly, you have a lot longer to perfect those skills/products over later entries into the market. Over the eight years I was in employment, I had numerous offers because my skills were ahead of the curve.

The best job I had was at a Design Week top ten agency. This was, by far, the most significant time in my short employment career. I worked with some great people on some great projects. It was the dojo where I learned a whole new set of skills. Karate Kid I was not, but I can look back and see many "wax on, wax off" moments. I was essentially pushing pixels around the screen for senior creatives. Through this process, I learned a few things about kerning, letter spacing, and vignettes to name a few.

Away from my screen, I became aware of a whole new depth to my thinking. A creative seed that was about to break the surface and grow rapidly. I began to understand that there was more to "design" than graphic design, which up to that point was my only, and blinkered, view of design. Once my vision for design had expanded, I found myself being a major contributor to design challenges, especially where late 90's tech was concerned. However, as good as that was, it came to an end. Sadly, they closed our office and let us all go.

A Free Lance for Hire

I didn't have time to dream about a future business—at that point, my dream was the job I was in. So once that final meeting had been called, I went out onto the street at lunchtime and called a few contacts. I remember it being a bit like that moment in *Jerry McGuire*. When he's about to get sacked and he's trying to make calls to get clients. But in my reality, I was standing outside the bakery. In a cloudy northern city with a sandwich in one hand and a mobile phone in the other. Much less Hollywood, but I did call my contacts and launch my new freelance design service.

I freelanced for three years and then briefly took a full-time position with one of my freelance clients, before realising a "job" was not for me. A small taste of freedom was all I needed and I knew I wanted to be my own boss. After leaving that position, I promptly set up my own limited company, a real business.

I took all of the skills from my previous roles and employed them to work for myself. When I look back at those negative words spoken by my teacher, so far he's been correct—I haven't become a car designer. However, my passion for cars has led me to design car wraps for Motorsport and the Gumball 3000 Rally, which have been featured on TV. I have worked with an electric car startup and my designs have sat in BMW showrooms. That's the closest I've come to designing cars so far. However, I still have time, so if anyone knows Ian Callum, I'm up for the challenge if he is.

Designing with Big Stuff in Mind

In the latter part of my design journey, I started to work in interiors, collaborating with interior designers and architects to create interesting spaces. Many of these spaces have been in healthcare, and I've seen the positive effects that environment can have on patients. This, in turn, created my love of psychology. Psychology is always part of a designer's life—it is in the way we design products to be informative, to be functional, to be "lovable", or just to be plain saleable. In my business today, I try to focus on the customer/user experience and how that impacts the customer's feelings towards products or brands.

Designed to Stick

I have been in business for over twelve years now, during which I've had many ups and many downs. I'm not a superstar entrepreneur who has made billions, but I am a

guy who at 13 had a dream about what he wanted to do—
and went out and did it.

I am the owner of a design company, that mainly designs
with stickers in mind. I've shipped millions of stickers over
the years, huge stickers for buildings, medium size stickers
for major car brands, and tiny little stickers for well-known
games companies. I've worked with some of the biggest
and coolest brands in the world. I have had emails from
celebrities asking about our products. I've had phone calls
from TV companies asking how we could help with the
'opening shots' of a TV show. I've had my work featured
on several TV shows, even making a short appearance on
60 Minute Makeover myself. My products were in the BBC
World Service lobby and I have shipped them all over the
world. I've had a skate legend drive around in a vehicle I
designed and wrapped. I've installed graphics in virtually
every major hospital in the UK, impacting thousands of
people's lives.

And I'm still in business when the stats say that only 10%
of businesses make it to ten years, I think this is because of
my passion for what I do. I say all this not to brag, but to let
you know that you can do the equivalent in your own
business too.

Overall, my life satisfaction is nine or even ten out of ten.
There are days when I have to do things that I don't enjoy,
but I'm so glad that I'm doing this "unenjoyable" work for
ME and the progress of MY company, rather than for
someone else. I love what I do, which makes life so much
better. This is why you need to create some action steps
and make your dream a reality.

All of what I've just relayed - my life and my design experience - has created this book. I hope you enjoy it, but most of all, I hope you get something out of it. I wrote it to be purposeful, to help those who want to be entrepreneurs and small business owners. The book is about creating the dream you want, and creating it now. Not tomorrow.

So on with the book bit...

The Business

The following chapters are practical ideas on starting and running your dream business.

ONE

First Things First

So how do you get from your dream to reality? Whilst I am a dreamer, people would say that I'm also a practically-minded chap. If you want to achieve success, your dreams have to at least start out with some sense of practicality.

In the first chapter, I'll show you how I would test a dream business scenario. We'll see whether there's any semblance of it actually being around in a few years. We'll consider whether it could make a living for the dreamer, as the reality is that the dream will become a nightmare if you can't make money from it.

Vision

Firstly, you have to clearly define the dream. Imagine you loved baking and you had always dreamed of starting your own little boutique bakery. The fun part is thinking up what you might do. How will you deliver this skill, product, or service? Then you need to come up with the name for your idea. We'll assume that you already have a good idea for the name. However, we will touch on branding and logos in greater depth a little further on in the book.

So let's start with the simple process of writing a statement about your dream, like this: "I am the owner of Daily Delights, a low-calorie cake delivery service" (insert your name and service of course). Does this fit you? Do you like it, does it make your mind race, or does it fill you with dread? Is this really the dream? Writing it out often crystallises the fact in your mind. If there is a hint of doubt, maybe you need to tweak it and think about it a little more. Then read on...

Secondly, set yourself a goal that is achievable. That doesn't mean sell yourself short and pitch low. It means *be realistic*. I often see people reacting negatively towards small goals or dreams. However, we're not all going to walk on the moon. Some of us are content with conquering Everest. Some are content with climbing Mount Snowdon. Others are just happy climbing the hill outside their town.

Whatever your dream is, I caution you to be sure that you have the desire and the ability to achieve it. Sadly, statistics tell us that the dream can often become a nightmare, swallowing your finances and sometimes your sanity. I'll come back to this subject later, as audacious and risky dreams do have a place in the entrepreneurial journey, but for now, you need to believe you can achieve your dream.

Creating achievable goals needs a little thought. So using Daily Delights as our example, let's walk through this. Say it's April and you're still working at a clothing retailer in a busy town. Your goal might be "By Christmas, I want

4

Daily Delights Deliveries to have five businesses signed up". That seems a reasonable time frame to get the business underway. You have some time to save for the equipment. There's time to design a logo and promotional material. And you have time to canvas local businesses and get feedback from a handful of them.

Practical Reality

This is where the dream meets reality. With every dream, there needs to be a reality check, and this is usually done in that dreaded application: "the spreadsheet". Let's look at the figures first. Assume you have five medium-sized businesses on board, and you find five regular customers from each business who want to buy your delicious cream cakes every weekday. You could roughly estimate £2 per customer. That's 5 x 5 x 5 x £2 so a total of £250 a week, which is not likely to be enough to start a business.

So, you need to look at methods of increasing the amount of customers and also the price of the product. You'll need to target a sixth business, and create a scheme that gets one more customer per business. So that's six regular customers per business. Then you increase the price to £2.50—after all, you do make the best cream cakes around! And you've figured out that the best price is actually is £2.50 considering your raw material costs, time to prepare, and delivery costs.

That makes 6 businesses, x 6 customers, x £2.50, x 5 days a week. That's £450 a week. £1800 is looking better for the first month, but it's probably still not quite enough to cover your monthly mortgage/rent and bills.

To ensure you have enough income, can you expand to a nearby town to find more customers? You can, but you'd need some help to service the nearby town. Whilst it would mean more sales and more money into the business, a large chunk would be going back out in wages. People are the largest cost to most businesses, so try not to employ anyone until you really have to. In the early days, minimising the stress on your outgoings will be a priority.

So, to get a reasonable income, you need to aim to sign up ten local businesses, with at least six people in each business who are prepared to buy your epic cream cakes every day. They're low-calorie cakes, so don't worry about them over-doing it!

10 businesses, x 6 people purchasing, x 5 working days, x 4 weeks, x £2.50. This works out at £3000 in your first month.

This figure could signal a "quit your job moment". If quitting your job is your aim, then you need to get those people signed up. That means having their signature on a piece of paper—not a vague "Yeah, I'd buy one". That kind of verbal commitment often spells heartache, as it can end up in a no sale later on.

Asking someone to sign paperwork makes them properly consider what they are saying. If they can't afford £12.50 a week for cream cakes, they will more than likely withdraw before signing. There's also a psychological play here, as people like to be consistent with themselves. If they give their word, they like to keep it. So signing a piece of paper makes that commitment more likely to become a reality.

Be aware, there will be natural fallout from your customer

list, especially if you don't have the product in front of them there and then. As a result, you may want to aim for eleven businesses, so you have a contingency if some people pull out at the last minute. These are the kinds of things you need to think about before taking the plunge with a new business venture.

Knowing Your Numbers

This book applies equally to those who have taken the plunge already. Sometimes, people jump and try to assemble the plane on the way down. As an example, I once met a woman who decided to start up a business. She had quit her job and borrowed some money from family to buy the kit she needed. She had enough left to tide herself over for a while. I referred work to her, as she did to me. Then one day she asked whether I would invest in her business.

I was flattered, of course, but I instantly flipped into "business mode". I asked her "What is your profit like? What are your costs? How much do you need to make to break even? What is your hourly rate?" All I got back was a worrying collection of "umms" and "ahhs".

As it turned out, she didn't know these crucial elements of the business. I'm no mathematician, but understanding your business numbers is fundamental to *actually having a business*. There is no "business" if you don't know the numbers—you merely have a hobby that sometimes pays. Sure enough, the business was gone in a couple of months and she went back to working for someone else. Her idea shone brightly for a moment in the sky, only to be as fleeting as a firework. But it could have been different.

I was once thinking up a new idea with someone and doing rough numbers; it looked great in theory. Then I started to dig into the "practical reality". How did we deliver this service, and so on? I am generally Mr Optimistic, but when it comes to business, it is better to be Mr Realistic. So before I knew it, I had broken what had seemed a perfectly profitable idea. To which the other person said, "Why do you always do that—try to look for problems?"

The thing is, when assessing a new business idea, you *should* try to break your dream, try to break your goals, try to break your numbers, or try to break your plan. If it survives, go ahead and build a business that thrives. If not, then it's time to rethink.

Key Points

When I start a new venture or idea, these are my benchmarks and key pointers:

Know your dream - Do you love it? Are you good at it? Can you achieve it?

Know your goals - Create goals based on a practical reality. Can you bake enough cakes in your oven? If not, best budget for a new oven.

Know your numbers

• How much do you personally need to survive at home? •
What are the costs of any materials?

• What is the cost of doing business?

• Do you need to pay money out to someone to trade?

• Add all that up -can you make a profit?

• Have you allowed for a contingency?

• Overestimate the losses and underestimate the wins.

Know your plan - So you know your dream, your goals, and your numbers and there is a valid business there. Now you need to create a plan of action. How are you going to market your new business? When are you going to market your new business?

Execute the plan - Once you have the plan (this is the crucial bit so don't miss it) GO AND DO IT. Do not procrastinate any longer. There will never be a perfect day. You will probably never have enough saved up to see you through. And in reality, not having any money is a pretty big motivator for executing the plan.

In summary, step up to the diving board (check your dream, goals, numbers, and plan), then dive off and execute the plan.

Checklist:

- Outline your dream.
- Create practical goals.
- Understand your numbers.
- Create an action plan.
- Execute the plan.

TWO

Sidepreneur

In the last chapter, I told you to dive in, which is a pretty craaaaazy thing to do if you don't have all of your ducks in a row first. I had to do that when they closed my office and some people actually love that kind of pressure and often thrive as a result. However, a fair number also crash and burn. So if you're not quite brave enough to go banzai and quit this afternoon, you can dip your toes in the water by becoming a sidepreneur first.

A what? I hear you say. Being a sidepreneur means being an entrepreneur on the side, whilst keeping your regular job. This is something that could be permanent or a way of testing your business idea before going all in at a later date.

There's not a big difference between getting started with this and creating a normal full-time business. You still need to know what your dream, your goals and your numbers are. If you actually want to go full time eventually, you'll need to work this aim into your plan. Do you want to use evenings and weekends to build your business? Or is this just extra cash that you'll use to increase your standard of living? Are you hedging your bets for a bit of income security with a view that this side business will never replace a full-time job?

The difference with "sidepreneuring" is that you don't usually have the luxury of creating a business that requires a physical task. You could be a window cleaner in the summer months after work. But by late September, there will be little or no light on an evening. This is why most side projects are digital, because they can be done remotely. Freelance graphic design, copywriting or web design are probably the easiest kinds of side business to start with, as they require little or no overhead. The only energy costs would be heating and light. You'd be using these anyway watching TV if you weren't the motivated entrepreneur you are! You could also start a business from home in the evenings, selling something over the phone or the web. You could post items in your lunch break or better yet, have someone like Amazon dropship them for you.

The Darkside

There is a darkside to this gig though: being a sidepreneur can be exhausting. Imagine you have just done eight hours in your regular no-hope-for-promotion job, then you get home, you have your tea, and you're right back at it. At first, you don't care because it's your baby and you love your new business. But at some point in the next few months your website is going to crash, or one of your clients is going to need something urgently and you may need to pull an all-nighter! Then you have to either call in sick or go into work, where you will be no use to anyone.

Then there's the sidepreneur widow or widower, the one who sits idly next to you watching TV whilst you get on with your business. You know the person, the one who sleeps in your bed and speaks to you for all of ten minutes a day. Being so preoccupied with your sidepreneuring can have a very negative impact on your home life.

Then there's the "oh no, the boss is about to find out" moment. I experienced that when I was doing a 9-5 and freelancing on the side. I'm not sure whether this was a contractual "no-no" or just a company-wide social "no-no". However I was asked by a friend of a friend whether I wanted to design some graphic panels for an exhibition. This was easy work to do on evenings and weekends, so I accepted it.

I went to see the designer and started to have a mild panic attack as the meeting went on. I found out it was for a project my employers had pitched for and not won. But being a bit naive and hungry for work, I took the job anyway. The graphics were part of a bigger project my employer was handling. So it meant that in my in my 9-5, our project manager was passing me my own artwork to check and approve before I sent it to link with the rest of the project. Talk about high blood pressure! I felt sure someone was going to notice something.

So, if you want to ensure you're not risking unemployment by being caught in the act, check your contract.

. . .

Things to Check

There's also this nasty thing to consider called tax, urgh! You might want to brush up on tax, or get a good accountant. The last thing you want is a hefty tax bill when one of your clients gets audited and the tax man follows the invoice trail. Don't be a gambler—I know people who regret having ignored this vital point.

You may also need to look at your home insurance. Your current insurer may not cover you for running a business from home. If you're renting, your landlord might not be too happy to see a million tie-dye t-shirts hanging from the rafters. All these things sound obvious, but it's always worth looking at the possible negative outcomes before you dive in. Any adjustments required should be covered in your numbers and planning stages.

With those risks considered or plainly ignored, the life of a sidepreneur can be good. You get security, but get to do your own stuff too. Lucky you!

The Numbers

As with running a full-time business, you need to know your numbers. Likewise, if you have plans to go it alone at some point, you need to ensure you build your side project big enough to support you as quickly as possible, which also means knowing your numbers.

If you're running a service business on an hourly rate, like a designer or bookkeeper, one thing you need to consider is: when working out your hourly rate, you might think "Well my wage covers my outgoings, so everything else is gravy". You may think you can afford to keep your hourly rate low to get more work. However, if you want to go full time with this side project at any point, going in too cheap could make that very difficult.

It's crucial to figure out the amount you need to pay your bills—to keep the wolf from the door. Then add a little extra for contingencies, like the washing machine blowing up. Maybe add in a nice holiday to Italy. Once you have your total outgoings, take that yearly figure and divide it by 48 weeks.

I say 48, not 52, as you'll be on holiday for two of those weeks in Italy, and there's also Christmas and other holiday days you won't want to work. Then divide this by however many hours you would want to work in a week if this was your full-time occupation. If you want to work 9-5 for five days a week, then divide it by forty hours. However, maybe your ideal scenario is to work less, so divide it by 20 or 30 hours. The figure that's left will be your hourly rate. I would then round up a little.

Example:

£14000 a year for rent/mortgage

£8000 for food

£4000 for rainy days & contingencies

£1500 for nights out or whatever you need to live happily

£2000 for a nice holiday in Italy

Total £29500

. . .

Divide the £29500 by 48 weeks and then by 40 hours. This is £15.10 per hour. Let's round it up to £16 per hour, which is the minimum you should charge.

This is your minimum hourly rate, even if you are only doing it as a sidepreneur on evenings or weekends. When you have this number, you can discount your fees/costs to get a client, but knowing *your real number* is paramount.

As a sidepreneur, you might think that's a lot of money you're charging and will mean you won't get much work. However, it's better to value your services correctly now, whilst you have a steady income, rather than find out you've priced yourself too low when you do go full time. Doing so can mean you fail to meet the rent or ultimately go bust.

Being a sidepreneur for extra income, it's easy to have a pricing issue that you cannot see due to the fact that you have another income from your job to support you. The prices you set might not be sustainable and would cripple your business if you were to go full-time. So be objective.

Having too many side projects is an issue that I'll discuss in the "Less is More" chapter. When considering side projects, I use the same process shown in the previous chapter to check the value of them. A side project does allow you some freedom that you cannot get in a job.

Summary

A sidepreneur business is just like any other business. If you want it to be successful, you need to make sure you know the fundamentals.

- What is your dream?
- What are your goals?
- Do you want to go full-time with it someday?
- What are your numbers like?
- Can you make a living from it if it's your only gig?
- Do you have a plan?
- Do you need to put certain things in place before committing to it?
- Can you make it happen—is it a real option?
- Is there a plan to throttle back the hours if family or work life suffers?
- Are you ready to execute the plan?

Checklist:

- Outline your dream.
- Create practical goals or next steps.
- Understand your numbers.
- Create an action plan.
- Execute the plan.
- Avoid the darkside.

THREE

Products

Imagine waking up in a luxurious hotel in the Mediterranean, your phone bleeps and you see you have another sale of one of your products. The panel in the app swipes open to reveal that this is your best month yet. And all this time, you have been on holiday.

This is the dream, but most of us start off being paid hourly for what we do. So how do we achieve this dream? This chapter is all about creating "products" from your current skills that help achieve your goals, whatever they may be.

Inventing a world-changing product might actually be what some of you are dreaming of. Whilst we will touch on that kind of product, the real value in this chapter is for people who sell their services by the hour. These people can unlock their time by creating a product. That doesn't necessarily mean the kind of product that is made in a factory in China. What it means is creating or designing an item just once that you can then sell duplicates of. This could be anything from videos to designs, photos, written words, or courses.

Selling Time

When I was freelancing for other design agencies, I sold my time by the day. I would either be given a figure that equated to the number of days the project would take, or I would have to estimate the amount of time required to complete the project. When I started working with local companies, I had an hourly rate, as the projects were much smaller. The main problem I encountered was when my estimation was well under the time it actually took, or when there were lots of amends.

If the problem is selling time at a fixed price, increasing the price might be an option. The other option is to speed up and still charge the full amount. I once accepted two pretty big projects simultaneously. For the first few weeks of the projects, it was great. However, as they both neared their completion date, it all got a little bit stressful. This is where creating a product is often less stressful than selling your skills for time.

My New Product Idea

With some inspiration from my friend Guy, I created a wall sticker product that I could sell online. I built a website, created a couple of dozen designs and then sat back and waited for a sale. In a month the sale appeared on my website. Then more. And more. Before we knew it, we were in magazines, papers, and blogs, and my products were on TV shows.

The beauty here is that when I was selling hours, I constantly had to keep designing to make money. But now I could design something over the weekend and stick it up on the website for it to be bought by one or hundreds of people. In return, all I had to do was send a file to the cutting machine. I spent no more than 5 minutes on an order. Needless to say, I loved it. My phone would ping all weekend and when I went in on Monday, there might be thirty to forty orders at an average value of £50 per customer. I could make more money whilst I was surfing at the weekend than when I was freelancing for five days a week sometimes.

Package Hours into a Product

Now, let's think about how you might be able to do something similar. You might think "That's all well and good because you had something that you could make, that was a product, with a box and instructions and labels, but I'm an accountant—how do I make a product?"

Well, in every business and industry, we usually need to create some form of value to exchange for cash. In the case of accountants or professional services, it may seem difficult to move away from the hourly/daily rate model.

If I was working with an accountant, I would ask this question: Do you need to sell your service by the hour? I imagine they would respond with, "Yes, how else will I do a customer's accounts?" That is where the problem lies—the old model of thinking is that you can only make money from doing the accounting.

What if you could create a step-by-step video series that talks SME owners through bookkeeping, helping them keep on the right side of the taxman? Would that course have any saleable value? Of course it would! You may need to find a good place to market it and you may need to help and support people. But just imagine what it would be like if that video course was £150. And you sold 30 over a weekend? That's £4500 over a weekend whilst you are visiting family or taking a break in New York.

You could also package up some how-to booklets and templates to sell from your website. You might offer a bookkeeping crash course for five people at a cost of £300 PP. That's £1500 for doing 4 hours of work, teaching four people, but saying the words only once. Then you could coach other accountants to teach it. You could write a book and sell it online, or actually get it printed and sell copies. You could try to get speaking gigs that in turn help you sell your products.

Or let's take another profession, being a writer. A writer may still wish to write for clients and even charge by the hour for this service. The key is to think outside the box and create repeat income from work you do once. Jon Buchan, a brilliant copywriter I know, once used to sell his copywriting in blocks of time, if not by the hour. He tried out an idea of packing up his knowledge into a subscription service and it started to work. So much so he didn't need the agency model of time for money anymore. All he does now is market and promote his writing course whilst trying to improve it and make it better.

. . .

Location-based Products

"Ok, that was easy", you might say, "Those are services that can be digital. How do I make a product? I'm a dog groomer! I have to actually groom the dog to make money".

Let's start easy and build up.

Start by bundling your time into a package. For instance, if it takes you an hour to groom a dog, and most customers are within ten minutes' walk, you could offer a "Collect and Groom" package. That way, the owner doesn't have to worry about dropping off their dog. The price would be double your groom rate or hourly rate for a fractional increase in your time.

Then you could train others. You could do grooming classes for owners like "how to keep your dog's coat looking great". Or for other groomers starting up, outside of your area, of course. You could create an information product that people could buy, such as a book or booklet on "the best grooming techniques to keep your dog's coat shiny". You could create a physical product, such as a branded dog brush that you sell in the shop and online with a 60% margin. You could even create some special doggy treats for those lovely owners who can't resist treating their dog.

Then move on to higher values services. You could add a photo service, where people can get their dog groomed and photographed. Like those photo studio offers in supermarket lobbies. People use dog sitting and dog day care services and charge for those - do you have the space and staff to expand your offer? Or what about a doggy retreat? A nice weekend away with a handful of your clients and their dogs to walk or enjoy dog-friendly beaches. You could charge handsomely for this by including gourmet food for the dog and owner. Then you can even do a little masterclass on some dog whispering techniques.

Sometimes it's hard to fully extract yourself from having to do something by the hour. However, if you can add products that sell whilst you sleep or bigger ticket items like retreats, then you could build enough revenue to employ someone else to do the hourly rate work for you. This would give you more time to enjoy life away from work or to develop other product ideas.

Digital Products

There is, of course, the digital world of apps and web products that could make you staggeringly rich overnight. There's a bit of luck to this though, especially in apps. No one can predict what's going to be a hit or when. If you haven't already built a huge hit app, it's getting much harder to get into this space. However, it's not impossible. With some hard work and some "growth hacking", which is another term for creative marketing, people are still making significant amounts of money from their bedrooms.

The value of a digital product is often in the unseen part of the business. Things like user numbers can make you very rich if you want to sell the app/product to another company. This is about the value of the customer base, rather than the amount of sales you make. If you're going to build something digital, like an app or web service, it might cost you a lot of money before you make a return.

I once designed and built an app that I assumed I could monetise after it had reached the point of success. We had over ten thousand downloads of the free app and had plans underway to build the pro version when the costs started to outweigh the values. Launching an app is one thing, maintaining an app is another. Android and iOS are constantly updating and this in turn can break certain things within apps so they need to be updated. Couple this with the fact that there are a significantly large number of devices and user skills out there, so the negative feedback can roll in pretty quickly when things break with major operating system updates. It is always worth budgeting more than you think for these kinds of products.

Products in an Internet Age

For those of you who actually have the dream of creating and selling a physical product like I did, there is no end to the options. You may not have a digital product, but the reach of the internet supplies everything you need to build that product. There has never been a better time with crowd-funding options such as Kickstarter and Indiegogo. Once you have a price for developing the product from your manufacturer, you can start a campaign to raise the cash. With some of these platforms, if your campaign can't raise the money, you have no obligation to take the idea further and you are left with little or no loss.

For example, Blaze (www.blaze.cc) initially raised £50k on

Kickstarter to make their bike light, which is now sold nationwide in bike stores. In 2015, they had revenues of over £1m.

I can't say this enough—there has never been a better time to design and launch a product. The cost of design and marketing is virtually nil compared to what a major brand would have paid ten or twenty years ago. 3D modelling, 3D scanning, and 3D printing make rapid prototyping as easy as popping down to where the photocopy shop used to be. When it comes to actual production runs, sourcing manufacturers in places like China has become accessible to small business owners and even sidepreneurs. Bedroom entrepreneurs making millions reselling products from Ali-express are not uncommon.

Dropshipping

Or you could use someone to dropship your products, and a dropshipper is only a web search away. If part of your dream is to have a line of printed t-shirts, there are plenty of folks out there who can take all the hassle away from you. All you do is send them the order. They print the t-shirt to the correct order details and ship the item. You take all the cash up-front and pay the dropshipper at the end of the month. You can do this for a host of services too. You may be an interior designer that wants your own branded range of chairs. There are people who will produce and dropship furniture for you. Your job is getting the customers to sell it to. We'll cover some of how to do that in the following chapters, but it is something you can do from a beach in the south of France.

. . .

Out-of-the-box Thinking

Turning your by-the-hour skill into a product could make you money whilst you sleep, play, or laze around on a beach. If you want to think outside the box, here are a few starters to get you thinking:

- Could you start by bundling your time into a more profitable package?
- Could you train/teach others?
- Could you create an information product?
- Could you create a branded product to sell online or in stores?
- Could you create complementary higher value services?
- If you are local, think how it is done globally. If you are a digital product, think how can you deliver this physically. Switching perspective should bring new insights and ideas for growth.

In my story about freelance graphics and stickers, it taught me that I am actually better off *not* selling my design skills by the hour. I was better at using my design skills to sell my own products. Consider whether this is something you could do? Take your core skill and use it to make your own product or business different and better.

Summary

With the above questions applied to your business, maybe

you can find something that no one else has thought of yet. Packaging your time as a product could allow you to make more money. Or if you create a digital product you could even do less work, for more money! In the Internet Age, the capabilities to manufacture your physical products are a click away. And access to a global marketplace is also only a click away. So if you can create the right product, maybe you can be sitting on a beach whilst your empire of products sells in the background.

Products are the way forward.

Checklist:

- Package time into a product.
- Think outside the box.
- Create a physical or digital product.
- Add "High Value Extras" to existing core skills.
- Think of alternative ways to launch your product.

FOUR

Branding

This chapter is all about turning your dream into something tangible. You have your business idea, but how are you going to sell it? How will people know who you are? The first step in this process is to select a name, and from that name, a logo.

Logos are a funny thing really. With just the application of a logo, the cost of a shirt can double. The quality of a service can be deemed more valuable, and a car can be seen to go faster. In reality, that might not be true, but that's often how we perceive it. In this chapter, we'll look at how this works and what you can do to get your dream off on the right foot.

When a visual logo or icon is consistently positioned alongside a high-quality item or outstanding service, that icon becomes synonymous with the value of "quality" or "luxury". For instance, Ralph Lauren can put his logo on a perfume bottle and the value of that perfume is much higher than equal contents from another brand.

All because of the logo. This logo only has the perceived value of "quality" due to the consistent quality of Ralph Lauren's apparel.

Of course, the opposite is also true. When a logo is consistently associated with poor service, the logo or icon immediately becomes equal to that service. I won't give an example for fear of being sued, but I'm sure you can think of a few! As you can see, the power of perception is a key tool in making your business stand out above all of your competitors, and that all begins with your branding.

History Lesson

We'll start with a brief history of branding. You can probably guess where the use of the word "branding" comes from, but you might be surprised to know that it goes back much further than cowboys driving cattle across America. Back as early as 3000BC, the Egyptians used branding irons to mark their livestock. The Romans continued this, and even marked human slaves. The English used branding in the Middle Ages to graze cattle on common ground, which eventually spread to America, Australia, and the rest of the world in the days of the British and Spanish empires.

Thankfully, the modern-day version of branding is not quite as brutal. More than just a mark or logo of ownership like it used to be, branding has become all-encompassing. It is about customer experience, communications, company vision and story, and even the unseen elements of the business. Each area becomes greater than the sum of its parts, turning a soft drink company into a brand or a mega-brand like Coca-Cola or Red Bull.

Now for a quick lesson in Ancient Greek, we find the origin of the word "logo". The word "Λόγος" or "logos" translates to "word". So, the logo of a company is literally the word that represents them. For example, Coca-Cola's logo is the word "Coca Cola" in a scripted font. Google's logo is the word "Google" in blue, red, yellow, and green. Pretty much every major brand today uses their word as their logo: Facebook, Sony, Ikea, eBay, Nike, Tesco, and Disney.

Some brands also use icons alongside their word, such as Red Bull. Their logo is the word "Red Bull", with an image of two charging red bulls against a sun or yellow circle. Similarly, McDonald's uses the word "McDonald's" and a yellow M icon, which is also known as the "golden arches". The "golden arches" were originally real arches, which were part of the restaurant design, they are now one of the most recognised symbols in the world. They represent the consistent service you can expect from a McDonald's anywhere in the world and shows the importance of getting your logo right.

Copyright and Trademarks

As logos are so recognisable and inherent to a brand, most major brands ensure their logos and symbols are protected by law with what's known as the "trademark". The trademark is said to have first been used in the days of the Roman Empire, when blacksmiths marked a symbol or their initials into the handle of a sword. This practice of marking metal goods continues today, where craftsman or jewellers mark precious metals with their own "hallmark".

A trademark means that, legally, nobody else can use a company's logo or symbols on their products or services without the company's prior permission. Whilst there are a number of protection types that I won't go into here, I will give you a few examples that you should probably investigate for your own enterprise: trademarks and wordmarks.

For one part of my business I registered the trademark of the visual logo to protect unauthorised use of it, and this trademark mainly protects *the visual look* of the logo. I also registered the "wordmark" to protect the use of *the brand word* without my authorisation. When I write the word out in text, I add the ® symbol at the end, so that other people know it is protected.

The Importance of Good Branding

Branding has been a love of mine since the age of 13, when I decided that I wanted to be a designer. I was a little bit of a geek and collected Coca-Cola cans and memorabilia—such was my passion for big brands and logos. Fast forward ten years and I ended up working in a Design Week Top Ten design agency working on global brands such as Nestlé, Lego, and Vodafone. When running my own company, I created numerous brands, products, spinoffs, and side projects for myself. This is where I learned some important lessons in getting the branding right when you start out.

If you have already built a multi-billion-dollar business, feel free to disregard everything I'm about to say! But if you don't have deep pockets, getting it right first time might be the most important thing you do for your business.

It's hard to analyse the impact of branding on your new startup or business; however, if you look at the established brands, you can quickly see how a major branding error can cost millions. Remember the new GAP Clothing logo in 2010? That escapade is estimated to have cost GAP $100 million!

So, maybe the reason you haven't moved forward as planned *isn't* because your sales team aren't working hard enough. What if it's because of your logo and branding? Will your branding cause the slow death of your dream?

Let's move to a more positive stance, how to create a memorable brand...

Where to Start: the Name

It all starts by naming your product, service, or idea. There are numerous conventions for naming companies and products, so I'll briefly run through the most popular types, in no particular order.

Names

Personal or family names tend to be used for older companies, often in serious professions such as finance and law. Fashion brands often use the designer's name, such as Ralph Lauren, DKNY (Donna Karen New York), and Calvin Klein. Adidas is a compound of a name: Adi (short for Adolf, his first name) and Das (short for Dassler, his surname). Ford and Disney are also family names.

Keywords

There is a strong convention of using a clear keyword in your name to denote what you do. For example, Pizza Hut, Burger King, and PayPal—there's no mistaking what area of business these companies operate in.

Portmanteau and Compound Words

Another naming convention is portmanteau (blending two partial words or sounds) or compounding two full words—pushing two words together to make one new word or name. For example:

Netflix (InterNET FLIX slang Movies)

Microsoft (MICRO-computer SOFTware)

Walmart (Sam WALton MARkeT)

Nescafé (NEStlé CAFÉ - French for Coffee).

Words with Meanings

Words with obvious, hidden, or abstract meanings also feature a lot as company names. For instance, you probably know that Nike is the goddess of victory, but did you know that Amazon.com was going to be named Relentless.com (try it)? The name was changed to Amazon to denote its scale, as the Amazon is the longest river in the world. Other brands like Apple and Orange have stories and meanings too. Similarly, Ikea is an acronym of Ingvar Kamprad (the founder), Elmtaryd (his farm name), and Agunnaryd (the village where he grew up).

Create a New Word

Sometimes brand names are created that sound like something else. For instance, Rolex was famously created to sound luxurious. Similarly, there are others like Häagen-Dazs, which was made up to sound Danish. And Kodak was completely made up by George Eastman, the founder, and his mother. Arguably, the most famous intentional misspelling—Google—comes from the mathematical word "googol" meaning equivalent to ten raised to the power of a hundred. There are many others, especially in the tech startup world, such as Zappos, now owned by Amazon, which is a creative use of the word "zapatos" which is the Spanish word for shoes.

Creating a Logo

Once you have your name, then you need to create a logo. This may be as easy as typing the word out in your favourite font. Think of the simple logos of SONY and Panasonic. You can also include visual elements such as symbols, which we'll discuss further on. Some logos feature hidden visual meanings, such as the FedEx arrow between the E and the X, the CBS eye icon, and the Amazon A to Z arrow/smile.

Next, you need to consider the colour of your logo. This is a hugely complex issue with links to specific industries and psychology. Colours are often subjective and cannot be detached from a personal perspective. For example, if blue is your favourite colour, you will have a different experience of blue to someone whose favourite colour is red. Studies have shown that colour plays a part in purchasing decisions. As such, you could just choose your favourite colour and ignore all of that, but you might be missing a trick! If you have a fun brand, use red, orange, or yellow. If you want to be trusted in finance and law, then consider using blue or grey. Green is synonymous with natural products and peace, whilst purple is seen as creative and imaginative.

On the flip side, choosing to use a colour outside your industry's convention could get you noticed, like Hermès Paris. Hermès is a luxury high fashion brand that uses a cheerful orange whilst their luxurious competitors use silver, gold, or black. However, be careful when doing this as it could do the opposite to your desired effect.

The following is a list of colours and their commonly-perceived values:

Black: Luxury, authority

White: Purity, clean

Grey: Neutral, calm

Green: Growth, health

Blue: Dependable, strength

Purple: Imaginative, wise

Red: Youthful, bold

Orange: Cheerful, confidence

Yellow: Clarity, warmth

A Picture Says a Thousand Words

If you look at 90% of the world's major brands, they use symbols called "brand icons". You may want to create something in your logo that has a visual meaning related to what you do. For instance, Burger King's logo features a burger bun around the text, and the e-commerce platform Shopify uses a shopping bag icon. Other brands approach this slightly differently. For example, Jaguar Cars, Shell Oil, Taco Bell, Apple Computers, and Pizza Hut all feature icons or symbols. However, their icons are based on the abstract element of the name - jaguar, shell, bell, apple, and hut - rather than the product they sell.

There are no specific rules in logo design, but it pays to consider your logo wisely. We process pictorial information 60 times faster than text, so it's surprising that few global brands choose to use a symbol showing the product as their icon. Pictures transcend language, especially given that we live in a global marketplace where our customers speak many languages. If you go to Tokyo and see a picture of a burger with some Japanese text, you'll instantly understand what the business sells.

The Professionals

As a designer myself, it would be odd for me not to have an opinion on using professional graphic designers to do your logo. However, I really don't want to be too closed-minded about this area, so I'll put it this way: you can do it yourself, using Word or Paint, and create your brand. However, like any profession, using a designer gets you past a lot of the guesses and incorrect moves. A good designer understands the subtleties of what fonts and colours convey to the viewer. A good designer knows how to appeal to the eyes of a customer. A good designer tends to have years of experience and feedback from professional training, but also real-life projects, where they have fine-tuned their skills.

Like any sector, you can pay lots of money for design skills or you can pay next to nothing. And like most professions, the more you pay, the greater the skills and knowledge you get. However, there are always exceptions, like the GAP example earlier. Within design, there are lots of people who *can* do logos. However, not all design is created equal, so here is an example of what you can expect to get, roughly in order of price.

<u>DIY logo</u>: Free and quick. Personal understanding of the business, but not necessarily the ability to communicate that.

<u>Online tools</u>: Cheap and quick, but no personal understanding of your business. Purely based on the visual appeal and your ability to choose correctly.

<u>Web design companies</u>: OK to good. Often limited interpretation to just screens, not always transferable to print, signage, or other mediums.

<u>Signage companies</u>: Cheap, quick, and tailored to you, not often transferable to digital formats like web or social media.

<u>Marketing companies</u>: A more intellectual interpretation of your brand. Usually with quality design.

<u>Graphic design companies</u>: Usually the best for small businesses. Logo tailored to your specs, with experience in

what works, to create a good-looking brand across various media.

Branding companies: The specialists. They understand your business sector, creating stunning visuals and a brilliant intellectual interpretation, often at a significant price.

It's always worth remembering the adage "you get what you pay for".

An example of the value of branding is one of my neighbours Croots, who make quality leather goods and bags. The business had been going years, ticking over slowly, creating a living for the owners and their staff. The business was then purchased by the daughter and son-in-law of the founder. They went on to spend a significant amount on re-branding the business to pitch it at a different market. Today, that business sells their same high-quality goods and bags in Harrods and Beams in Japan. Of course, there was a lot of hard work that went on behind the re-brand, but if you want to play a bigger game, your branding has to be at the higher end of the spectrum.

Remember, you get what you pay for.

Summary

Let's recap. First, you need a name. Then you need a logo, with an icon or without. Then you need your brand colours. Once you have those aspects in place, you have your visual identity. You could choose a professional designer to create these with your input, and then protect them with trademarks and copyright.

In the 21st century, we need to take a wider view of what "branding" means. There are other areas where customers interact with our company that become synonymous with our "brand". This includes things like the frontage of our shop, the cleanliness of our offices, and how we or our staff answer the phone. It includes the way our emails look, our spelling and grammar, what our timekeeping is like, and whether our packaging is appealing. All of these things add up to how we are perceived by our clients and customers. The power of perception is a key tool in making your business stand out. This is also what we call "branding" in the modern era of business, so we'll touch on some of these considerations in the next couple of chapters.

Checklist:

- Decide on a name for your business.
- Create your logo (and icon) or get a designer to do this.
- Think about your brand colours.
- Get your logo protected by copyright.

FIVE

Visual Assets

In the previous chapter, we covered the logo and determined some colours we can use with our visual assets. Visual assets are anything that represents your company/service in visual form, such as an advert, a van livery, or a social media banner. I love this part, as it's one of the most important aspects of getting your brand right. Your visual brand goes ahead of you into the world. It appears in places where people have never heard of you—places where they can't talk to you about your brand values or how you do business. It's a visual representation of *who you are*, and it may be the only interaction that some people have with your company.

As I mentioned in the last chapter, people read pictorial information far quicker than they can read text—so quickly that it's down to the millisecond. However, people also make judgements about you and your company in seconds, two seconds in fact. In his book *Blink*, Malcolm Gladwell talks about how we make snap judgments in the blink of an eye. This term is called "thin-slicing", and it was first used by Nalini Ambady and Robert Rosenthal in 1992 in the *Psychological Bulletin*. Thin-slicing is an unconscious skill that we use all the time to make sense of our world. As Gladwell puts it:

"We thin-slice whenever we meet a new person or have to make sense of something quickly or encounter a novel situation. We thin-slice because we have to, and we come to rely on that ability because there are lots of hidden firsts out there, lots of situations where careful attention to the details of a very thin slice, even for no more than a second or two, can tell us an awful lot." (Blink: The Power of Thinking Without Thinking, 2005)

Therefore, ignoring this in-built human trait could be a disaster for our businesses. However, we can also use it to our advantage. When I worked for a design agency that dealt with some large corporate brands, we were always given a brand guideline document. These guidelines showed us the way we should use their logo or visual assets. And why would they do that? For the **consistency** of the brand. In this thin-slicing world, brand consistency triggers an unconscious association with the product.

We also see skate or surf brands use the opposite of consistency to give their brand an "edgier" or "anti-establishment" feel. They achieve this by having several versions of their logo, no corporate colours, and no specific design style. Don't for a second think that this is haphazard —with the big skate brands, this is carefully considered to create the feelings they want their customers to feel. It's a corporate identity where much craft and skill has gone into making it look *unlike* a corporate identity.

. . .

Getting the Look Right

If you sell organic fresh foods, using a strict capitalised logotype (font) may not accurately represent your company. Something like handwritten script seems to be more relevant. Equally, if you're in the legal profession and you use Comic Sans, apart from the fact that your designer needs shooting, you're unlikely to get any work. Your profession shouldn't be jolly and fun, so neither should your font. When you get things wrong in the legal and finance sectors, people can go to prison, so a traditional font may be a better solution to display your seriousness and accuracy.

In most towns, there are many small businesses who choose to adopt the consistent branding methodology, which is good. However, there are others who have one logo font on their building signage, another font on their vans, and a totally different one on their staff clothing. It may seem like I'm being pedantic about graphic design, but in reality, we're all making subconscious judgements about businesses like this. Our subconscious may recognise these inconsistencies and translate that into unease about the company. The question of whether we buy from that company or another down the road could be made on a tiny unconscious snap judgement, or thin-slice, about the company's branding, consistency, and presentation.

Think about it like this: your company may have the best stock in the world, or you may have the world's most likeable salesman, but people simply don't come into your office or shop because they think your company is terrible due to poor branding. You may well be the best at what you do, but you need your potential customers to see that, or you'll never get the opportunity to show them.

Digital Assets

Now we'll look at some of the places where we typically use logos or visual branding to represent our companies. We'll start with the online world and then turn our attention to the physical world.

Whilst this is about the visual aspect of the web and social media, it's crucial to have your domain and social media usernames all locked down. We'll cover that in the next chapter.

When you're developing your logo idea with your designer, it's always best to keep in mind the place where most people will view it. If this is online and on social media, you probably want to think *square*. Not square as in boring, but a square format, rather than landscape or portrait. Most icons for social media are squares or circles, so try to keep your logo readable in a square format. Stack the words on top of each other, or try to keep the text bold so it's readable as a small image. If you can't do that because your name is long, then your supporting visual icon needs to do the work. Make the icon strong and obvious—and stick with it. In time, whatever it is, it will become associated with your brand through repeated association, which we'll look at next.

In addition, when you're populating social media, such as Facebook or Twitter, these platforms have a place for a header image. This is an important visual asset that should communicate something about the company. For example, it could be an image of your latest work and/or exterior or interior shots of your offices. There is a caveat to this: only use good-quality photography. If potential customers visit your Facebook page and see amateur or poor photography, this could create a negative judgement in their mind. If you're not very good yourself, get a photographer. You can also use the professional shots in your brochures and adverts. However, if you have a good camera and fancy yourself as a bit of a photographer, then it would be useful to do a quick course on Udemy or Creative Live. In the worst-case scenario, go to YouTube and search "how to take great pictures", or something similar. Whatever you decide, make a considered effort, because those header images represent you and your brand.

Consistency

As I just mentioned, over time your logo will become associated with you, so you should stick with it. This is down to that visual reaction time—all the skills and positive memories we have about a brand flash through our mind when we see a logo. Assuming that your customers value you, if you change that logo, you're often removing that association, as many major brands have experienced. The same goes for social media. My advice to clients is to always maintain the same icons—don't keep changing them. If you really must fiddle with your profile, just change the headers, and not the icons.

Consistency over social media is important too. Use the same icon on all platforms. If I go on Twitter and I see the same icons as on Facebook and Instagram, I know who I'm dealing with. If you change it or have different icons on different platforms, I may assume it's another company, a fake account, or worst of all, I could just ignore you completely. I believe this should apply to personal accounts too, especially if you're a celebrity or Head of Industry—keep the same headshot so we know it's you; it will become your icon or logo.

In the Real World

I already mentioned my pet hate of inconsistent signage, but having been part of the signage world for a time, I know that signage companies sometimes get poor quality and inaccurate artwork files, if they get any at all. So let me be clear, it is *your job* as the business owner to make sure your brand is consistent—not your supplier's job.

Whoever creates your logo, be it a highly successful design agency or your local sign company, they will be able to supply you with a digital and scalable version of that logo. I know when starting out that there is often a temptation to keep costs down by creating your own logo in Word or Paint. However, unless you are actually a designer, this is not your job. It is your job to be the brand guardian for your company and it is your job to hold the digital copies of your branding. It's an important job, as important as having the keys to your office! Unless you have these files, you can't be consistent across all the different media you will need to promote your business, such as advertising, exhibitions, web, press coverage, clothing, merchandise, building, and vehicle graphics.

. . .

Signage

Occasionally, when I get on my soapbox in the studio talking about signage, I'll trot out lines like "the purpose of signage is to communicate", which in itself seems an obvious statement. Of course, a sign is supposed to communicate, but *what is it communicating?*

Is it communicating through words? Or is it using images that display the information in a quick and clear way?

What does a wonky logo on the back of your van communicate about you? What does a small and illegible telephone number do for you?

My personal advice on buildings and vehicle signage is to K.I.S: Keep It Simple. Use clear, concise wording with an image that communicates what you do and your contact details.

Does that mean you have to be boring? No, not at all. Be fun, be outlandish, get noticed, but always remember to consider whether your customer sees it the way you do. Wrapping a van in beautiful images ensures the Sky vans are noticed. Eddie Stobart's branded fleet of wagons is a national treasure to anyone with kids on long journeys in the UK. They are obvious and they stand out. But wrap your fleet in something that doesn't exactly fit your image, and you could be undoing any good work you've already put in to developing your company and brand.

Summary

To recap: think about all of your visual assets such as your logo, company colours, uniforms, vehicles, signage, website, social media, and advertising. Are they representing you accurately? Do an audit to find out by asking other people. Task a designer to correct any perceived inconsistencies and weak visuals. Make sure you do not neglect this very public-facing aspect of your business.

Checklist:

- Look at other businesses and think about your perception of them.
- Research how people perceive your brand.
- Create quality visual assets for marketing online.
- Create consistent quality visual assets for signage and print.
- Be the brand guardian.

SIX

The Web and Social Media

Now that you have your name and your logo - with or without an icon, and in the right colours - you need some presence. And where better to start than with the web and social media? However, this is where things get tricky. If you have chosen a common or obvious name for your company, you may struggle to secure a unique online domain or username.

Imagine if "Apple" was the name of your Dental Surgery —it's guaranteed that you won't get the name "Apple.com" as a domain name or as a username on the internet anywhere. So you need to box clever and use other means. For instance, you can add the product type to the domain or username, such as AppleDentalSurgery.com. Or you can add an action as a prefix, for example, GetShinyTeeth-AtApple.com. Or add a location, such as the suffix "UK" or "London", for example, AppleDentalUK.com. The key thing to remember is *the shorter, the better* when it comes to domains.

The same applies to usernames on the big social platforms, where your desired name may have been taken already. This is tough luck really, as there's little you can do to retrieve these usernames from people who had better foresight than you. I know because I've tried, officially by emailing Twitter to ask for a username, and unofficially by offering the holder money to get the username. This is despite owning the Registered Trademark for that name. Again, you have to play the same game with prefixes and suffixes until you find a username.

When doing this, I recommend you spend time aligning your username game, for that important reason we talked about earlier—consistency and being recognised by your customers. Don't use a hyphen on one site and an underscore on another. If you can get the name you want on Twitter, but not on Facebook or Instagram, stop and try again with a different version of the name. I recommend only choosing a username that you can get on all platforms.

Take note! Make sure you register your username on every new app or platform going forward with that same name, even if the app or platform turns out to be a flash in the pan. You never know which platform might be the next Snapchat, Twitter, or Facebook, so grab that username early. Make good use of username and domain name checking tools like Namechk.com.

Dominate

Another tip on domain names: a prominent SEO (Search Engine Optimisation) expert once told me that I should register as many domains around my niche as possible. Owning these domains helps stop your competitors from ranking better than you. Sadly, in my case, the major keywords connected to my niche were unavailable on .com and .co.uk, but I still managed to snap up several other major domains, and I still have them protecting me today.

If you can get keyword domains in your niche, point them at your brand website. You can do this through domain forwarding in your domain tools, but a quick search online will inform you. It's a bit like buying up all the shops on a high street and therefore not letting your competitors steal any sales. By all means, do this on social media too, grab your keyword usernames before your competitors do. For example, I have three accounts with similar names, but I only use one. On the other two accounts I have a post that tells people to follow my main account. This stops anyone else registering them and making better use of them than me.

Websites

What you decide to do on the web and social media will be based entirely on your business. You might need a website to sell products on, or you might need a one-page website asking people to sign up with their email address. You might just need a simple holding page, or a brochure website. Each business will have very different needs and processes. However, there are a couple of key things to remember when building your website or social media content. Ask yourself the following questions:

• What does the customer want?

• What is my competition doing well?

• What is my competition doing poorly that I can excel at?

• How can I make content that expresses the company ethos?

• How can I make content that builds my relationship with the customer/client?

• What content can make us more visible and shareable?

• One of the fundamentals to any website is: what does the customer want and why do they need/want to go to your website?

Question Your Motives

Some people design their website to save themselves time, making the customer put in lots of details, but others realise that the easier you make it for your customer, the more likely you are to make a sale. Are you making it easy for your customers? It's always worth questioning your motives when it comes to your website. You should throw out anything on your website that doesn't have value for the customer. Making them fill out a 20-question sign-up form so you can segment your customer market is not a benefit to the customer. However, if that sign-up form allowed you to provide them with a significantly better service, you could possibly justify it. The main thing is to treat others as you wish to be treated yourself. If you don't like filling in forms, don't make your customers do it. Make their life easier.

We won't go in depth on UX and UI, but a book on the

subject, *Don't Make Me Think* (2000), offers this key tenet: "don't make your customers have to think about an action on your website". This is crucial to your website, which you can check by asking someone to test out your website whilst you watch. If you see them hesitate, then you're probably going to lose customers. Putting barriers in the way and making a customer hesitate for even half a second is likely to end in a negative experience.

Social Media

So your website is sorted. Now let's look at social media. We're all familiar with social media and we're probably familiar with the various kinds of content we should be posting. There are no real hard and fast rules, because every time there is, someone comes along and breaks those rules and makes a killing.

However, in my opinion, the best kind of content to feature on social media fits into these categories:

- Show off your skills/products
- Show your passion
- How-to's
- Behind the scenes

The first one is the easiest, because if you're selling a product or skill, you usually have something to talk about.

Showing your passion is a little harder for some people, especially those who are not in a passionate industry. However, you still need to talk about your passions. I know someone who is killing it online because they **love** their product—and nothing sells more than customers seeing people who are really passionate about what they do. Sometimes this person even shows the product too!

The third way, *How to do X*, is a great way to solve a customer's problem. In the case above, the guy talks customers through various ways of using the product. The "How to do X" type of post can also show off your product, and display your passion.

Finally, the behind-the-scenes pics and videos are a great way of building a relationship with your customers. Everyone likes to peek behind the curtain.

I often write a big list of social media topics and ideas first, then when I have 15-30 I will start writing posts or collecting images. I then use software such as Buffer or Grum to create the posts and have them post at a future date. Using scheduling tools like these means you can allocate a period of time to the task of social media rather than trying to post manually every day. There is further advice only a search away about the frequency of your favoured social media. If I was to opt to manually post on a daily basis, I would often forget, and one key thing the experts say is that consistency of posting is crucial.

Do's and Dont's

When writing content:

- Do stay on topic.

- Do stay niche—be the big fish in the little pond.

- Don't try to appeal to everyone.

- Do stay clean, there are cases where swearing and nudity get you likes, but for most businesses, you should avoid this.

- Do be regular, keep posting, and keep blogging.

- Do like and comment on positive comments.

- Don't start fights. On social media, negative comments escalate very quickly to name calling, so avoid the temptation to get involved.

- Do post quality content, double-check your spelling and grammar, and only post great photos (as mentioned earlier, hire a photographer or take an online photography course).

- Do use hashtags.

Hashtags

Hashtags - you mean those things that young people use? Yes, I do. Here's a geeky little fact. The hashtag is actually a labelling system used in computer programming since the 70s. However, back in those days, they used the £ symbol to denote a label. Even when it was the pound symbol, it was still called the hashtag. The modern version of the social media hashtag came into being in 2007 on Twitter. Think of hashtags like a "label" search engine. Today, most of the major platforms support hashtags, which means we can use them in our tweets, pictures, and posts to label the content we're producing. Then anyone interested in that kind of content can easily find your posts/tweets.

Now you know that hashtags are just labels, you can search for popular hashtags and add them to your posts. That way, people looking at the hashtags you're using will see your content.

When using hashtags, avoid trying to cram a billion highly popular but unrelated hashtags into your text. This might get you a like or two, but it's unlikely to get you followed—and building a "following" is what you want to do on social media. The best way to start is by trying to find posts by people in your niche, especially influencers (I'll explain this shortly). Take note of their hashtags and the number of likes and comments. Then click on the hashtags and search through all the other content labelled with the same hashtag to find other related hashtags. Then repeat the process. Be aware, you can go off-track with this tactic, a bit like those videos on the sidebar of YouTube, so it's worth keeping in mind *your particular content* so you can get back on track quickly. However, don't be afraid of throwing in a slightly wider audience hashtag now and again.

I'm all about the examples, so let's take a look at one. As I'm writing this, #coffee has 61 million posts on Instagram. In the 6+ years that Instagram has been active, that's approximately 9.5m a year. That's 26k a day, 1000 an hour, 18 every minute. Given that the growth of Instagram has largely been in the last two or three years, that number could be way larger per hour right now. So if you post a picture with the label #coffee, your post is less likely to be seen. This is due to the regularity of new content with that same hashtag, which pushes your post down and out of sight.

Using an obscure hashtag has the same problem, but for the opposite reason. Say you used the label #coffeecumbria

—your content might stick around at the top for a while because hardly anyone is using that hashtag. However, the fact that hardly anyone uses that hashtag means no one will find you.

The upshot is you want a hashtag that's not so unpopular that you're never found, or so popular that you're never seen. The only way to find this type of hashtag is to test and measure. **Test and measure** is my favourite process, as I'm creative with a side order of technician. The "creative" proposes the question or test, then the "technician" measures the results, and the process becomes an endless circle of improvement...in theory anyway.

If you're not wired like that, there's another option. It's called... **spray and pray**. In this method, you just find lots of hashtags in your niche and try them all out in posts. 30 hashtags is the limit per post, which means you might have to mix them up with each post. Over time, you can see which work and which don't.

Before you get too far down the rabbit hole of likes and follows, ask yourself what the purpose is of these posts. Likes and fake followers are not the point. The point is to create a genuine following of people who like your stuff. This happens through creating regular and great posts. Once you have that foundation of great content in place, use hashtags to get the audience for it.

Social Signals

Earlier in the chapter, I mentioned influencers. Influencers are celebrities, athletes, tech gods, or YouTubers. They are people who have a massive following on social media. If you look at their profiles, they normally have half a million plus followers, but only follow a few dozen people. In the landscape of social media, these are the accounts that us mere mortals follow. There is a social and a psychological signal here that says the influencer must be worth following, because everyone else is following them.

The opposite of that is also true. How many people have only a handful of people following them? The signal here is —they're not worth following.

With that in mind, you might have a great product, but no one thinks it's any good because we only have two dozen followers. So you may look to buy followers, which you can do via websites like Fiverr. These followers can then make our new product look as though you are followed by others, and therefore worth following. It is just like a queue in front of a night club, people only want to be where the crowd is.

The thing with paid followers is—they're not real people, so you can't sell your products or services to your fake followers. However, you can use the power of influencers to reach their network of followers.

If you are interested in these types of methods and want to get to the next level of social media, you can look into "growth hacking" tips online.

Easy Tips for Growth

Using the power and example of influencers, there are some simple hacks for your social media:

- Try to get social media influencers to retweet you.
- Try to get featured on other people's blogs.
- Celebrate your products—don't oversell.
- Post pictures of your happy customers.
- Follow the right kind of people and influencers.

Who are the right kind of people? It's worth following the movers and shakers in your industry, though they don't actually buy from you! It's the regular person who is looking to buy what you are selling. But how do you know who they are? They're the people who are following your competitors. Follow and interact with people who have just followed your competitors on social media, as this usually means they are in the research phase of a purchase. When you follow them, guess what? You suddenly pop up on their radar to be added to that research phase. Like that, you just upped your chances of a sale.

Be a Flexible Closer

You can build a cool website or system that makes it easy for you to do business, and have the best social media presence. However, new customers might not want to do it that way—they may want to call, message, or email you. If you reply to their email or call with "go to our website", I can almost guarantee you've lost the sale.

Be a flexible closer. Have your pricing structure and FAQs ready in an email or document that you can paste in response to them. Most customers want the basic data, but if they are messaging you, they likely looking for reassurance too. Make them feel you're a safe bet. Be friendly, not robotic—do not auto-respond to these messages. This is the key point in a sale and anything you do to spook the customer here means you lose.

Finally

This chapter could be a hundred books in itself. However, don't let this side of things put you off starting a business if social media and the web isn't your strong point. The web and social media are vehicles to help you promote your business—just like the local paper or advertising. If you lead with passion and just keep the quality high, you will win some ground online. Metrics such as traffic, likes, and followers are great but they can become a distraction in themselves. The reality is—we want people to buy something from us and that is always the main goal. You don't need to discard the previous information, but don't become overwhelmed by it all.

Checklist:

- Domain and usernames should be consistent.
- Solve your customers' problems.
- Don't make them think.
- Test and measure. Test and measure.
- Make sure you're visible. Hashtags can help with that.
- Social signals can be faked.
- Don't get overwhelmed by it all.
- Show your passion.

SEVEN

Company Ethos

Now you've created a logo and brand identity, we'll expand on some elements we touched on in the previous chapter. We talked about brands, but what makes a "brand" a "brand"? A logo on its own does not make a brand. A brand is something wider in scope, and is held together by intangible elements that we can't see or feel. The modern understanding of a brand is really the company/product ethos. It is what the company stands for, who the product is made for. You could call this "the spirit" of the company/product.

So how do we define the spirit or ethos of your brand? It all starts by understanding what YOU want. The great thing about starting a business is that you get to define what you want your company to be seen as. Do you want to be known as a cost-effective solution or a premium service? Do you want to be renowned for your professionalism or that you are down to earth?

There is always a trade-off, as you can't pick countless

things that you want to be known for. If you pick too many, you'll tie yourself in knots trying to stick to the company values—to the detriment of your productivity. It's better to pick three things at most that you'll be known for, and ensure you do them really well. If you don't, you won't be known for those things—you'll be known as something else entirely.

What Do Your Customers Think?

I'll tell you this little story as a warning about why it's important to do a few things well. I used to have a client whose larger projects I enjoyed doing. However, between the large projects, they often gave me some very small jobs —jobs that if I had the chance, I would have turned down. However, to maintain customer relations with them, I just took the jobs—albeit begrudgingly. This meant that the small jobs often got side-lined and ended up being last minute. With the larger projects, we were known for doing a great job, so I didn't consider the effect of these small and seemingly unimportant jobs on my customer's perception. It turned out that my client obviously didn't see it the way I did.

One day, a new customer popped in, who had been told by my client that we might be able to help. In the course of our conversation, it came out that the client felt I was "a bit scatty and disorganised". As you can imagine that stung a little, but due to the lack of care I had placed on these small jobs, I had created that impression of my business. So the lesson here is: *choose what you do, do it well, and stick to it.*

. . .

What Are You Known for?

To choose what you do and how you do it, you need to determine your values.

Do you want to be known for your punctuality, attention to detail, speed of delivery, cleanliness, or creativity? Do you want to be renowned for your customer care, products, openness, quality, or value for money? Your variety of products, skills, friendliness, vision? Your knowledge, scale, legal standing, adaptability? Your politeness, wisdom, systems, positivity, understanding, and so many more things?

Your values will be specific to your industry and also specific to you as the leader of that business. These are values your staff or sub-contractors may not have, so you need to ensure that it's articulated to them: "This is how we do things here".

Your industry may be accountancy, where having the value of creativity is not considered a good thing; whereas the value of professionalism is pretty much a standard requirement. You could have the value of friendliness in addition to professionalism, and that may set you apart from your competitors. That's exactly how I see my accountant. Having used three in my business life, I value the care and friendliness I get from the people we use now.

Once you have your values, you could write them into a statement that encompasses the key elements of what you want to be known as.

Brand statements can be something like this by Patagonia, the outdoor clothing giant: "Build the best product, cause no unnecessary harm, use business to inspire and implement solutions to the environmental crisis." As such, their brand is known throughout the world for its quality and for the company's position on the environment.

Ethics Are Your Choice

For Patagonia, ethics—how they do business—is an inherent part of their brand. This is their choice, but some industries must adhere to ethical standards, such as the legal profession, which does not have the choice. Whilst in most other industries, the ball is often in the business owner's court. It's easy to start a business and pay ethics no interest at all, but down the line, you may find that your business has deviated from your initial desires. As such, it's a good idea to write your ethical conduct in stone from the outset.

For example, one of my ethical standpoints is around not telling the truth. I was brought up in a way that frowned upon mistruths, so I would rather tell you how it is than lie to you. Either I messed up, or I will put it politely that you messed up, simple! I don't think that lying to customers is a great idea, and my clients know this. I've said to them "I won't lie for you, but you know I'll never lie to you".

Ethics range from social issues, such as how we respond to racism or discrimination, to how we deal with privileged data, how we treat our waste, and where our materials come from. In some cases, ethics means we might have to choose which types of clients we work with, and the ones we turn down.

Thinking about the kind of ethical standards you want to portray is a worthy exercise. What's more, these standards do have a benefit—they aren't just restrictions. In today's global economy, customers and clients are looking to do business with people who have the same values, and buy from companies who share their ethics. They aren't just looking for the cheapest products.

Charity Starts at Home

Ethics and how you are perceived as a brand also extends to charity. If you want to be seen as enriching your local community, your business may want to support a charity or create its own social programme that helps people locally. You could combine a bit of team building and marketing by helping out a charity such as a foodbank or a local cancer centre. You and your team could help by cleaning up rubbish from your surrounding area. Or do a charity fun run as a business.

Customer Care

Customer care is a make-or-break situation for all businesses, and should automatically be part of your ethos. You will have experienced bad customer care hundreds of times, so I'm sure no stories are required to outline what that means.

However, customer care is not just a job for the Customer

Care team—it is a core value that all team members should be great at, whether they are front-of-house or non-customer-facing. If your salespeople work tirelessly to get a sale, just one tiny slip up by accounts, design, or even the cleaner could waste all of that hard work. If an error occurs fix it as quickly as possible and if you need to, retrain people to the standards you require. The key is having everyone in your business understand how to deal with daily customers and have a way to deal with issues that occur.

Finally

Your brand goes way beyond your logo—it is your company ethos. "Ethos" is the Greek word for "character". It is the characteristic spirit of your company culture. "Ethics" also comes from Greek—it is the moral principles or values governing your company culture. So what are those? This is your opportunity to define what your company is known for, but it is always worth checking what others see your characteristics as. Are your customers dealing with a company that cares about their experiences, or do the customers use you only because they have to?

Checklist:

- Define the ethos of your company.
- Define the values you want to be known for.
- Decide whether you want a corporate ethics policy.
- Put customer care at the heart of your business.

EIGHT

Creating Experiences

Let's imagine you have set out the business you want, and the numbers it takes to run a successful business. You manage to get a friend in a top design agency to design your logo and help with your website. You have reached thousands of new customers' eyes and your first customer is about to make a transaction with you.

There are three possible scenarios from this point. The first is you fail to meet the client's needs and it's the worst first sale of all time. If that happens, don't be downhearted as this is an opportunity to look at the failure and do it better next time. Alternatively, you might have fulfilled the customer's need and provide what they wanted. You ticked all the boxes and there are no hitches. In this case, you deserve a pat on the back for getting it all together first time.

However, there's another alternative, which is what this chapter is all about. This option is about going the extra mile, *exceeding expectations*. It's about creating a customer experience that will last in their mind and get them talking about you with their friends or colleagues.

Going the Extra Mile

Where do you start with this? First, you start with the free and easy stuff, before you start outlaying cash on expensive gifts like a luxury car dealer might do. Free and easy comes in the form of attitudes and actions. It's easy to assume that you will always exceed expectations by being courteous and polite, but in reality that is "standard" and should be your foundation stone. Exceeding expectations in a retail scenario might be something like wrapping a gift, or going to fetch something the customer has forgotten, rather than expecting them to get it themselves. For example, in Waitrose, staff are instructed to show you the item you are looking for when you ask them. If you have an online store, you can put in a personal note to the purchaser. If you're selling a service to a client, you could have their car washed whilst they're attending a meeting in your office, or something equally "wowing". You can even do this with the tiniest of gestures.

A great place to start is by trawling through the recesses of your own experiences and picking out the times when a brand, shop, or service exceeded your expectations. A few years ago, I ordered a second-hand part off eBay. When the package arrived, I opened it to find a little note and a packet of Jelly Tots. The packet was creatively edited with a sharpie to read the seller's name. That small gesture has stuck with me for years. There was also no mention of it in the eBay listing, so it was completely unexpected.

. . .

Better Human Experiences

So how do we design better human experiences? It's actually quite easy to improve a situation with the smallest of tweaks, something we'll look at in the *Power of the Small* chapter. And it doesn't have to be grand gestures to change the perception of your business or service.

Even small businesses can do great customer experience. We recently moved house and my wife noticed a window cleaning van over the road. My wife thought maybe she should ask the window cleaners about their service. As it happened, they were just finishing packing the van and were gone before she had the chance to speak to them. A lost business opportunity that they never even knew about.

Or it was, until the very next day, when a smartly dressed lady with an iPad appeared at the door. The lady went on to explain that she was from a local window cleaning company and was just canvassing the area. Some of your neighbours use us like "Mr Smith" she said pointing up the road. And "Mrs Johnson over the road", at which point my wife realised it was the same company she had seen the previous day. After a few minutes, she had signed up to have the windows cleaned.

I didn't know about any of this until a few days later. My wife came into the room to tell me she had received a text from the window cleaning company that said "the window cleaners will be around tomorrow in the morning between 8am and 10am. If you'd like to reschedule this, please call the office". That text message exceeded our expectations as we had never had anything like that with our previous window cleaners.

Let's translate a few of these things into designed experiences—things that could help you in that dream business. Firstly, the van had a sign on it, which is advertising, but it also brings social credibility to the company as it's parked outside the neighbour's house. In this case, it sparked a reminder about a service we had not thought about.

Secondly, the cleaners were smartly dressed, whilst our previous cleaners were often shirtless on hot days. Whilst that might be appropriate at the beach, it doesn't look very professional.

Third, there was a follow-up. They didn't wait to see whether the van signage would pull in calls—they proactively went out and called on people.

Fourth, they used social proof again. We didn't know "Mr Smith", but we did know "Mrs Johnson from over the road" which meant we could easily ask our neighbours what they thought of the service.

Fifth, she had a sign-up form, she didn't just post a letter through the door or hand out a leaflet and expect us to do the signing up when it suited us. She actively but politely pursued a customer.

Sixth, they made it easy for us to pay. We could pay the cleaners with cash or cheque, pay by card on their website, pay upfront or in blocks, or we could set up a direct debit.

Seventh, they kept us informed about the progress of our order—in this case, the first time we could expect to see our windows clean. Lastly, they didn't disappoint us. They promised and delivered.

People-centric Methodology

Taken in isolation, some of those things don't appear to be designed, but as a whole, someone somewhere sat down and said "How can we do this job better?" Better than our competitors, but also better for our customers. They drew up plans to create a window cleaning company that, no doubt, is doing quite well from their efforts.

Applying the **people-centric methodology** to your dream business is really simple in theory, but in practice takes effort. Though I can assure you it is well worth the effort. The starting point is this simple thought: "How would I like to be treated?" If you're looking to start a garage business, visit other businesses on the sly and think to yourself "How could they have made this better for me?" Make up a catalogue of items that you want to include in your own business. Some things may be too costly to start out with, but as you develop, they will always be on your list of improvements.

There are a couple of other statements I use when developing an idea: "How can I help a customer without the need for a transaction?" This could just be a colour sample or an email newsletter that bridges the gap between my business and a potential customer.

I also ask: "How can I make people smile?" Exceeding expectations is a sure-fire way to make people happy and smile.

· · ·

The Customer's Shoes

Put yourself in your customer's shoes. As business owners, we often try to maximise profit and minimise effort, and the casualty is the service the customer receives. They have to make more effort to buy from us or they get less product/service for their money. Earlier I mentioned the book *Don't Make Me Think*. One of its defining themes that I now take into the real world of business is do not put barriers in people's way when they want to make a purchase. Make the process as seamless as possible for them.

Exercise

As an exercise, think of every way your customers come into contact with you. Is it on the high street, via adverts in the local press, through the post, by email, on your website? List all of these touch points, then list the reasons *why* they interact with your company. Is it to complete a sale, bring back a return, pick up a collection, open an account, check an invoice, or make a complaint? Then think of how you can make it easy, make them smile, help them for free, and make it better for them at each of these points.

Checklist

- Go the extra mile.

- Think about your worst and best experiences and respond appropriately.
- Make your business people-centred.
- Put yourself in your customer's shoes.
- Make life easy for your customers.

NINE

Marketing

We have talked about creating your business, your product and your branding. But a crucial element not to miss out is marketing your business. Throughout the chapters in the book there are a few examples of the things I've done to market my business. There are things like giving customised gifts and sending images I have altered back to a client. Then, when you get a warm lead and the opportunities arise, going the extra mile is part of my marketing strategy.

Those are forms of marketing, but they are probably the less obvious forms. You may be anxious about digital marketing or social media and want to know more about how to do those, so we'll touch briefly on these, but in a general view rather than getting into the specifics of certain platforms.

The Classical View of Marketing

The four Ps of marketing are Product, Place, Promotion and Price. Your skills may dictate what your product is. If you're a carpenter and want to build a business around that, your product is likely to be either goods you design and make, or a service you sell to clients (though it may not be limited to these).

Place is about understanding where your customers are. If you are selling wood products, going to a meat market is not likely to be a great place to find new customers. If you are selling your skills as a carpenter you may wish to only promote yourself locally so you do not have to travel.

Promotion is about how you let those potential customers know what product you offer. You may wish to put an advert in the local paper, or you may opt for a more focussed approach and target people in a trade magazine.

Price is where you position your product. Is it high-end and expensive, or is it a low margin and high volume product? This is also about how you create promotions around your price, for example, two for one, or even discount codes.

The Shortcut

If that seems like a tall order at this stage, I have a shortcut. This shortcut is to simply check out what your competition is doing. Where are they promoting themselves and what price point are they at? Once you have that data you can further develop and fine-tune your marketing as your business develops.

I have used this strategy to start all my new business ideas. We then used experience to modify and correct the process we assumed from our competition. For example, we priced one of our products based on what a competitor charged. However, when we ordered their product in an intelligence gathering exercise, we realised we were using superior materials, which cost us more, therefore we were giving away profit when we tried to price match. So we stopped trying to price match and started selling our product as a high-quality alternative.

We also followed our competitors on social media and signed up to their email lists. We can see the typical promotions they put on and how their overall strategy worked. Some of these competitors are well funded and turnover millions, so we assume they have tested their marketing and found what works and what doesn't. We're standing on their shoulders, but it is only a starting point. You will need to develop your own marketing voice and not be just a copycat.

We ordered products from all our competitors and used that experience to build a better product. We created packaging that actually improved the buyer's experience and we used our experience to fine-tune that even further. As an example, we ask our customers to share photos of their orders on social media. When those images started showing up we noticed that most of the photos were of the product still in the packaging. We then redesigned our packaging to feature our web address on the inside lid of the box so that customers' images featured our website and hashtag.

Formats

Back in the day, if you wanted to market a product to an audience you selected one of three methods: print, radio, or TV. Print was often the cheapest and simplest solution for getting your message out to your potential customers, which is what most businesses used. These methods were usually advertising promotions, which sold the benefits of the product to a vast audience in the hope that a small percentage would try it. Today, however, there is a vast array of alternatives that can help you get your message out. There is direct mail and specialist magazines, podcasts, and audio adverts on music streaming platforms. And social media, banner adverts, and search, or SEO, as well as bespoke video screen advertising (like in shopping malls or train stations).

It is hard to get your head around what the best medium is, but I have two contrary thoughts on this subject. The first is, look at your competitors and see what they are doing, where they are fishing for customers? The second is, where are they not fishing for customers? This could mean they have tried and failed to reach a market. Or it could be they have not yet thought of it and YOU could well be the pioneer who gets all the benefits.

As a simple example from my own business, we had some PR written for a product of ours, which we sent out to all the home improvement magazines. Our logic was that the product would appeal to anyone improving their home. We did in fact see sales swing upwards when we were featured in several major titles and even foreign press. However what actually took us by surprise was that when our product got featured in a gossip magazine the upswing was significant and clear. We had found a market who wanted our product, yet did not reach through the home improvement magazines.

Messaging

With the above example we're starting to look at the importance of positioning your product. Positioning can be done through words or images. Words can convey who the product is for or what the product does. And images use the visual positioning of graphics or other items to create association. For instance, putting an attractive looking chap in a suit next to a sports car would position your product to a particular target market. The target market may not be guys who have suits and sports cars, but it will likely be people who would like to be, or have, a guy with a suit and a sports car. Your message would be implying that with my product you can be or have that. Think of perfume adverts and wristwatch adverts, for example. They're selling the product through association with beautiful people or scenarios.

Most of us will likely set out without the need for such expensive visuals, but we still need to consider their association. Think back to the colours in the branding chapter - orange might not be the best colour for an accountancy practice. You could however use images of professional looking people to convey your seriousness.

The key to messaging in the modern era of marketing is authenticity and honesty. Do not sell your product as high-quality if it is not. You may initially gain customers but you will soon disappoint them and will usually end up with a poor reputation. If your service is not high-quality, but is simple and quick, you should lead with those messages. Nobody likes to be deceived and in the world of social media, your reputation can travel faster than ever.

Inbound and Outbound

Finally, a worthwhile distinction to understand is inbound and outbound marketing. Outbound is what we typically understand when we talk marketing. This would be advertising, PR and promoting the product. When you are focusing on outbound you are effectively shouting out to everyone to tell them what you can do or offer.

Inbound is where you create a great environment and welcome people in who know about you through your reputation. Inbound marketing will often be brand related, this is where you are crafting your reputation. You do this in part by delivering on your outbound promises - if you say you are quick and are, then you have delivered and your reputation grows for being quick. You can use social media to sell products, but social media is often an inbound channel. With it you are subtly crafting your reputation so that when the time comes a potential customer knows where to find you.

Summary

Inbound marketing for me seems like the easiest thing to do because I come from the branding side of business. Even when I was at the agency we rarely did anything outbound as we were not about sales, but more about meeting expectations. Therefore after years in business I know that promoting your skills or service is a core requirement of staying in business. The Field of Dreams philosophy of "build it and they will come" is often why businesses fail. There is no point in being the best if no one knows you are there, or that you can help them. The key to success is both outbound – telling people what you can do - and inbound – doing what you say you can do - well enough to grow your reputation.

Checklist:

- Consider the four Ps of marketing.
- Gather competitor intel.
- Build your own marketing strategy on top of that.
- Consider which formats suit you best.
- Think about you target market for customers.
- What messages are you wishing to convey?
- Keep in mind that both outbound and inbound marketing are crucial to business success.

TEN

Systems

You may be completely new to business, but I know you won't be completely new to business systems, so here's a quick refresher in case you need it. A business system can be something written down or verbally passed down. It's a uniform and consistent way of doing something—usually a procedure or group of procedures that have been tweaked and honed over time. A system can be something that is legally required such as a Health and Safety procedure, or it can be something as simple as where deliveries are placed in your shop.

The Way We Do Things around Here

Don't let high-sounding names like "systems" and "processes" put you off. Instead, simply think of it as "the way we do things around here", a term I've pinched from Marianne Page. Marianne was a senior manager at McDonald's, and she took her considerable experience from that role with her own knowledge and beliefs around keeping business simple and consistent to develop the system. She proposes making every activity in your business "simple, logical, and repeatable".

Whenever anyone talks about systems, McDonald's seem to pop up, and that's because they built their global brand on their systems and procedures. They have systems for cooking, managing people, planning...they even have a system for sneezing. Obviously, sneezing didn't make them a multi-billion-dollar global business. However, all of the tiny, seemingly insignificant procedures they train their staff to follow make a difference.

When I was in my early twenties, McDonald's was the gold standard of systems and people development, and today it is still just as praised.

Your business or service may be nothing like a fast food chain, but you probably have a number of systems and procedures, maybe dozens, some of them even for really small things.

Systems for the Little Things

We have a system for a little thing—our online sticker sales. In fact, it was totally invisible to me until I was talking to someone who pointed it out and told me how much they thought of the experience.

When an order comes in, we check the website and print out the order receipt. We then select the product from our files and print or cut it. Then we "weed it" (remove all the bits you don't want). Next we apply a special paper application tape that allows you to fit the transfer sticker.

We pack the finished product, plastic application tool, instructions, and the order into a postal tube. We print an address label and our branded sticker and place them on the tube. Then we place the finished order by the door for the courier, who walks in, picks the orders up, and sends them around the world.

Each part of that process has been fine-tuned over the years. We have also tweaked it in a natural way.

Little Cogs Turn Big Wheels

This is the kind of system that most small businesses have, and like us, they are most likely passed on verbally and never written down.

I always felt that systemising everything took some of the "art" out of life. The last thing I wanted was someone with a clipboard standing by my side checking I hit all the processes. In hindsight, I see great value in systemising. And why is that? Because it frees up your time to do the more interesting parts of the job, or go home at a reasonable hour. It could just free up time in your business to do more of what you enjoy doing, whether that's networking, baking cupcakes, or preparing for the next big project.

Systems are like cogs and wheels spinning away in the background, clicking into place when needed. Without them, we end up wasting time, and time is money! We also risk going around subjects over and over, without any time or cost savings.

. . .

Release Profit

Ultimately, systems release profit from your business. If you add up all of your time spent on the sales process, chatting to clients, sending emails, and so on, these are probably not fully costed. Wouldn't it be better to reduce that time cost to yourself by implementing a procedure for on-boarding new clients? You could have an email template already prepared to ask for people's information, then just add your warm, human sentence or two at the top. This would cut out a chunk of time spent writing the same email you wrote last week, and the week before that, with all new clients. You could also have a telephone script for the same purpose. And what about your internal meetings? You cover the same points at every meeting, so rather than meandering through the meeting, taking up needless time, you could have a structure that gets the job done in half the time.

There are great efficiencies to be had, and those efficiencies add up to CASH. Cash that you can plough into moving the business forward. And the more forward momentum a business has, the harder is to stop them.

Scaling Your Business

Another great thing about systems is *scaling*, and it's basically what made me change my mind about systems.

At the time, the business couldn't scale, because *I was the business*. I was the one with all the processes locked inside my mind. I was the one who did all the client tasks, the pricing, the meetings, the calendar, and so on. That isn't a scalable business, and neither will yours be if you don't get used to writing down "the **one** right way to do things in your business", then delegating this to your trusted team or freelancers.

There's only one way to cook French fries at McDonald's—everyone understands that, and everyone there cooks fries that **one** right way, with no exceptions. Can your business scale?

Control Freakery

My epiphany moment happened when I was at a business workshop, and got talking to the guy who was leading it. We were chatting privately about scalability and I said that I was struggling to grow the business because I was "kind of a control freak". He asked me to ask the question later on in the group, as everyone needed to hear it. Later, I popped the question in the group, and in two minutes, I learned something that would change my business.

He said (paraphrased a little), "You need to stop being limited by your control freakery. All entrepreneurs are control freaks. What you need to focus on is creating systemised assets, so you can get on with the task of running your business whilst everyone else is working their part of the system. You don't have to stop being a control freak—you just need to learn how to be a better, smarter control freak".

He also said, "We have assets in our business that mean if I couldn't deliver this session, there are audio files, videos,

PowerPoint slides, and a script. So this talk could be done by any member of my team if I had to pull out".

"We have a handbook that has everything in it on how to do sales calls and how to sign up a client. There are forms and brochures stacked in the office that any team member can grab and sign up a new prospect".

You can guess what I did that weekend—I created the handbook for my business. It has "how to create files", "how to prep projects", and even "how to name the files" (so it's easier to find them in years to come). It has health and safety documentation, checklists, and planners for staff to use. It's still a work in progress as new things come up regularly, or something still isn't obvious, so we do step-by-step guides and even videos.

The Handbook

The great thing about writing things down in a book is that if you take on new staff, everything is there for them to read. Then you can spend half the time talking them through things, which means you have more time to do the important stuff. And they will always have it to refer to, instead of asking you over and over how to do something. The book also sets a benchmark. Ultimately, the handbook becomes an asset, and should you be fortunate enough to sell your business in the future, it means that anyone can buy it.

The Marketing Playbook

Even marketing can have systems, you can have documents showing how to collect your client's important details and how to input it into the CRM package, which is crucial for marketing to them, and keeping track of projects. You can also have a checklist in your sales process. This minimises the "trauma" of cold calling by doing it in stages, for example:

- Call to ask for a name to send a brochure to.
- Follow up and check they got it.
- Follow up again and see whether they liked it and have any questions.
- Then offer a meeting, where we present what we do and leave them with our best practice guide.

At that point, if we still don't have a hot lead, we'll send them an email to see whether there are any projects we can help with. If not, we'll leave it for a while, then get back in touch.

You need to be ready with your website, brochures, and guides as people will take some convincing to use your service. Google even did a study on this, called the "Zero Moment of Truth". It talks about the 10.4 times on average that people need to interact with you and your brand before purchasing.

With online and social media, create a copy and paste library, where you can take all the frequently asked questions about delivery, pricing, or processes. When a customer emails or messages you on social media, you can be personal and friendly, then paste in the information they need without having to retype it for every enquiry.

. . .

Summary

To sum it up, write your systems down, or create new systems for things you do repeatedly. Keeping it simple, logical, and repeatable is the key.

Systems help you scale, freeing up your time to work *on* the business, whilst your team work away happily *in* it—doing everything to your high standard, and consistently.

Checklist:

- Create a list of systems to help you work faster and easier.
- Detail "the way we do things around here".
- Systems scale your business, so don't keep them locked in your head.
- Create a handbook for everyone else to use.
- If you have staff, ask them to add their jobs to the handbook.
- Simple, logical, repeatable is the key.

ELEVEN

Show Me the Money

You probably feel that the more money you have, the better life is, right? Well it is, but only up to a point. Researchers have found that at around 70k-80k, the satisfaction per pound/dollar starts to drop. This means that moving up the income ladder from 20k to 30k to 40k to 5ok correlates with increased happiness. However, when people reach the 70k-80k mark, their happiness level no longer matches the increase in income. I'll leave you to do further research on this, but know that money isn't the be all and end all.

I learned a lesson about money in my mid-twenties. I was asked to come in-house for one of my freelance clients. I considered it and said I would for £x (which was half as much again to what I had been on only a year ago). They said yes, and I was so excited about it. However, less than a year later, I quit that job to start my own company. Having more cash was great, but I found that if the situation isn't satisfying, the money means nothing. And it certainly wasn't as good as running my own business.

You might not have the same hang-ups about money as I do. You might think "Show me the money!", or you prefer to offer your skills for free because money just muddies things in your mind. The thing is, many people are either scared of money or put little value on it. If you are one of those people, how do you move out of that mindset?

The first thing is to think *practically*. Don't place an emotional value on a number. Instead, be matter-of-fact about it. Think: to survive another day, I need this, this, and this. The cost of paying for food, water, and clothing is X. The cost of having the equipment to carry out the business, heating, lighting, and rent/mortgage is Y. Add all this up for a year, then divide it by 48 workable weeks, then divide it by 40hrs or 30hrs a week, depending on your goal. That is what you need to charge *per hour* to survive, no less.

However, what if you spend a whole week trying to chase a client and have no chargeable work? Clearly, you're going to be out of pocket. Will you be able to pay the rent that week? If you don't have the funds, you will have to do double the work, or double your hourly rate.

What if you are super-hot at your craft, but still don't value money or don't need it? Rather than pitch low, why not quadruple your rates, pay your bills, drink champagne, and send the rest of the money to the dog's home. Getting your price point correct is a market question, as well as a personal one. It's not fair to others, who have lesser skills, if you try to compete for work at the same price point as them, so do not undervalue yourself. They'll never get enough work to feed their cats. So know your industry, and don't go in low, as it will be really hard to pull yourself up from a low price point. Start high and discount a little if people's eyes bleed when you tell them your fees!

Be Smart

So, you have your hourly rate or product price list sorted and you're about to make your first sale. There is a temptation at this point to just do the work and invoice, then hope they will pay you. They might. Or they might not, as I found out on a number of occasions.

So how do you protect yourself against this? Firstly, it's prudent to do some checking online before agreeing to work with a client. There are a number of websites where you can check the trading and credit worthiness of a business. If anything looks fishy, run a mile! If you've heard anything questionable about them, don't even entertain them.

I was once approached by a guy who wanted me to do some work, but he had a bad reputation, so I was warned. However, I was a hungry (read: *naive*) new businessman, so I thought I'd be okay. We did the first few jobs by cash on collection, with no hitches. I thought "What were all those people talking about? He's a nice chap!" More and more work kept coming in, and we switched to invoicing, because I could do the work, but not do the admin of invoices in time for collection. The first invoice was paid, so there was no cause for concern, and I only noticed when the bill was nearly £3000—at which point I politely put a stop on the work until the oldest invoices were paid. Then the work stopped and I never saw him again.

If you want to get your money at this stage, it involves a trip to the small claims court, but I never did that. It was such a head-mashing process for an arty-type like me, so I just let it go. He went bust shortly after and started again in his wife's half-sister's cousin's name, which was his standard mode of operation.

Let this be a lesson—if there is even a sniff of something iffy, leave it for someone else.

I also learned a little trick from an entrepreneur that helps to avoid this issue. Create a sign-up sheet or contract before you start doing business with someone. It doesn't have to be massive, but it does need to state the terms on there. *Your* terms, not theirs. Once they have signed it, any lawyer can chase your payment up should they default.

Getting the Money in

Invoicing can be a real pain, and sometimes you just want to do the work, then forget about it. However, it's important to raise the invoice the minute you've completed the sale or project so that you do not forget about it. Use one of the array of web applications out there, and get it done. Your cash flow is the lifeblood of your business. If for any reason the blood stops flowing, you risk the demise of your dream. This is why I love having an online store. You can get the money upfront when the customer pays with their credit card, then you process the order, and ship the item. This keeps your cashflow in good shape and there is no chasing bad payers.

However, even when you invoice immediately after the

work is done, some customers might not pay as quick as you'd hoped. When that happens, remember they're still your customer, and you may want to keep working with them, so a conversation should be had rather than a forceful letter.

I once had a customer who we did a few thousand pounds' worth of work for, but a few months had passed without much communication from them on their account, even after reminders and statements had been sent. It was my task to call them and give them an ultimatum to settle the account, which I duly did. When I put down the phone, I thought, "That is not the guy I want to be. Why did I adopt that attitude?" I wasn't rude, but I was quite stern.

So I sent flowers to the customer to arrive the next day. I included a note apologising for my stern tone. I also mentioned that I didn't want to be like all the other contractors, and I appreciated that she was just doing her job, but I didn't mention the money. The phone rang the following day—it was the account contact, who was thankful for the flowers and said the money would be in my bank in a few days. And it was.

There is a psychological law of reciprocation, which I didn't know I was using at the time, but I've found that it works in almost every situation. If someone gives something to us, we feel they should have something in return. So instead of immediately going to the "bad" or "mad" place to get what you want, go to the "awesome" place instead and see what kind of response you get. Remember, the aim isn't to lose customers, but to keep them and get them to pay up.

. . .

Risky Business

In business, there is always a risk that you'll lose customers. There are lots of risks in business, but "having a small client pool" can be a big problem. If you are relying on a couple of big clients or contracts, this can be seriously risky, even if everything looks great in the bank and on a spreadsheet. All it takes is one customer to move to another supplier and your idea could be sunk.

So, you need to spread the risk by either obtaining more clients, even if they're smaller than your main clients, or by finding new revenue opportunities. Can you sell your product to a different market, with fewer big clients? For instance, taking a B2B (business to business) product and turning it into a product for the B2C (business to consumer) market. These clients will then keep you going between the big projects or sales.

Targeted Action

Sometimes you can make twice the amount of profit selling one kind of service or product than another, but there may be a problem if the profitable work is less frequent. This might mean you chose to have a few less profitable products/projects that are more regular to cover your overheads better. You will have to use your best judgement when deciding at what level spreading the risk actually has a detrimental effect on your ability to do the work well.

Extracting more revenue from your existing clients is a much better method than creating a whole new product range with different customers. For example, we already had machines for printing stickers, so I created printed stickers for the home, businesses, startups, car fans, BMXers, and gadget lovers. That all sounds great, as I'm using the same machinery to sell to lots of different markets, thus spreading the risk. However, I realised that every time I started a new product niche, it had a completely different customer base, so we had to start at the bottom and build our following again. This means creating multiple Instagram, Snapchat, Twitter, and Facebook accounts for each niche, and advertising in many different places, from car shows to nursery exhibitions.

A better solution is to build one key audience and sell them other related products. That way, you only have to manage one set of social media profiles, which is a massive saving on time and cost.

A Better Business Model

The best businesses are those that can get people to *repeat purchase*. If you have to acquire new customers all the time, you are starting at zero with every customer. However, if you get a customer who can purchase from you over and over again, you don't need to build up rapport and credibility every time. You also save on the upfront admin of account creation, which makes the process more fluid.

As an example, my wall sticker website used to sell thousands of stickers for homes. However, the model had a flaw because people only buy wall stickers for their homes when they redecorate a room, which is every three to four years! So, I had to relentlessly seek new customers, which cost in terms of SEO (search engine optimisation), Facebook adverts, and so on.

I realised that a better product was logo stickers for startups and businesses. These have a similar margin and cost per purchase, but are better because many customers re-order their logo stickers two or three times a year to give away at events. In theory, that means a £50 purchase of wall stickers every three years per household customer, versus a £50 purchase of logo stickers three times a year, which is £450 over three years, and £400 extra for every customer.

If you're trying to develop a business with a long lifecycle, meaning over a year, how can you keep selling to those same clients over and over? Can you sell them other products? Can you fix or service the product every year? There are many different models you can try depending on the product you sell.

Spend It Wisely

Time is money. Sometimes, you actually have more time than you do money. In this case, you could spend your time learning a complementary skill that moves your business forward. Or you might spend your time doing something that costs you more money than you have, like taking your time to design a website using a free online tool like Squarespace rather than having a web designer build it. However, as soon as you have any money to spend, you should be outsourcing work that you are not already skilled in. This usually means paying someone to do it for you.

This can be staff, freelancers, or other service providers

like lawyers or experts. If you're no good at bookkeeping, pay someone to come in weekly or monthly to keep the books straight. If you don't know how to do SEO, pay an expert. If you're a top chef, pay someone else to wash dishes whilst you prepare food. These are obvious examples, but it can be difficult to tell whether you should outsource or not. So here are a couple of suggestions when you should:

- One, if it involves anything that will land you in court, you should outsource it to professionals. You need to take ownership and oversee it though, as it would be you going to court, not your lawyer or accountant.

- Two, if it's a task you don't enjoy and won't land you in court, you should outsource it. This includes tasks like cleaning, web design, servicing machinery, or cold calling.

- Three, if it costs you less to do than you can earn from doing it, you should outsource it. If a cleaner cost £/$10hr and you charge £/$100hr, you'd be daft to spend an hour doing your own cleaning.

Summary

Money is the most emotive subject I've come across. Everyone wants it to some degree or another. Many profess to not chasing it, but in reality, 99% of us are. Once you recognise that money is a resource to help you do more than just enjoy nice holidays and a new car, then you can start to see money as oil in the machine. Cash lubricates your business to move faster and further.

Remember, when you have piles of cash, you can do more

for others, you can help to fix hunger and poverty—it doesn't have to be all about you.

Checklist:

- Work out your numbers.
- Choose your customers wisely.
- Think about how you'll get the money.
- Have a wide pool of customers to reduce the risk if you lose one.
- Focus on one area and do it well.
- Consider your business model and market opportunities.
- Spend your money wisely.

The Entrepreneur

The following chapters are thoughts on the mindset and tactics you need as an entrepreneur.

TWELVE

Psychology

Psychology is one of those weird things we don't really want to think about. It's often associated with negative feelings and psychiatrists, but in this chapter, we're going to reclaim it for **positive thoughts**. Psychology is the science of behaviour and of the mind, or thought. Over the years, this science has documented many of the things we do as humans.

Firstly, as psychology is the study of *behaviours*, this means it is about things we already or instinctively do. We're not inventing anything new here—we're just using some previous knowledge to influence how we build our businesses.

Don't Make Me Think

Earlier, I told you about the book *Don't Make Me Think* by Steven Krug. The book is primarily about web usability design. However, the concept also applies as a fundamental tenet in all user design - online or offline. The basic premise is that if you make something that a customer has to think about, even for a fraction of a second, you put a barrier in their way. If you put a barrier in the way of a customer, you are significantly reducing your likelihood of a sale. So when creating anything, make the process as simple as possible. If you're in retail, put the best products at chest height or eye level. If you're a service business, make your interactions clear and simple. If you are in manufacturing, make samples so the client can see what they are getting. Anything that makes the customer less anxious will be a benefit to the sale.

Another of my favourite authors is Robert Cialdini who has written two really insightful books on the subject of persuasion, *Influence: The Psychology of Persuasion*, which has sold over three million copies, and his follow-up *Pre-Suasion: A Revolutionary Way to Influence and Persuade*. These are both great books to help you understand the impact of psychology in a business setting. I've condensed a few of his thoughts on making sales and pleasing customers, as there are some psychological behaviours you can use in this process.

Reciprocity

First of all, we'll cover my favourite—reciprocity, which I mentioned in the previous chapter. It is my favourite because it works. For years, I never even knew it was a thing. Reciprocity is the mutual exchange of something of value. From a business point of view, we can exchange a gift of some value in exchange for an order. This subject has varying levels of scale, very light grey at one end and dark grey at the other. For example, we may agree that politicians being wined and dined on yachts in exchange for favours in Government would be at the darker end of the spectrum. But where would a restaurant be on the scale when giving out after-dinner mints? The gesture is still activating the same built-in behaviour from us, which is that we feel obliged to repay someone if they give us something first.

In a restaurant study, the gratuity tip went up by 3% when a waiter added a single mint. Not a great deal. However, if the waiter left two mints, the tip quadrupled to 14%. When the waiter left one mint, walked off, hesitated, and then returned with the second mint and said "For you nice people, here is an extra mint", the tips went up by 23%! The influence exerted was not just in *what* was given, but in *how* it was given. The key to reciprocity is to give first and make sure it is personalised and unexpected.

This really works, even when you don't realise you're doing it. A few years ago, when I didn't know about reciprocity, I created bespoke products for some UK based startup brands that I knew were attending a show I was visiting. On the day of the show, I hand-delivered the product. Some of the recipients were a little baffled. Some were, to be honest, a bit dismissive, giving a "Who are you to print our logo?" type response. A few were bowled over by it. One of these people was a big deal in the gaming world, and we chatted about ideas for ten or fifteen minutes and kept in touch for a few weeks. That interaction didn't turn into a big project, but I know the gesture sowed a seed because I recently caught up with them at an event we were both at and they still remembered me.

Sowing the Seeds of Success

This approach is a bit like farming—you have to sow seeds, and whilst some don't bear fruit, when one does, it will pay the costs of all the other seeds. That is exactly what happened—I managed to get the product into the hands of someone who cared. They passed them on to the right person in their company and we got a sizeable order from a pretty big name in enterprise technology, a company owned by Microsoft. From our initial investment of time and material, we made a 1000% ROI. The products were unexpected, personalised, and given first without any obligation attached.

So you can use this concept to your advantage in your new venture. Send a well wishes card to your customers on a date that is out the blue (not at Christmas, as that is expected). Don't advertise yourself in the card, just say that you value them or even a simple hand-written hello. Even if you put no sales pitch in it and you'll be surprised by the response.

If you are in retail, greet people with their name, give them a free taste or test of a product, and make them feel special. The owner of my local whisky shop, McMillan's of Malton, does this to great effect—he knows his whiskies, but best of all, he knows me! Once he even walked up the street with a little taster because he saw me go into another local business. Do I buy from him? You bet I do. I'm a fan for life!

. . .

Likeability

The owner of the shop I just mentioned also uses another key psychological tool to disarm his customers, though I doubt he sees it as that. That tool is *likeability*.

Likeability is a fundamental human behaviour. We like people who are similar to us, who cooperate with us, and who pay us compliments. Starting at the bottom of that list first, we're all aware of the people who are disingenuous with their compliments and we can grow to dislike people for that. However, more often than not, we are suckers for flattery, even when we know it not to be true. Often, the basis of this acceptance is whether we like the person doing the complimenting, and the compliment itself.

Secondly, we like people who cooperate with us. This is a logical, almost animalistic trait. In the book *Sapiens: A Brief History of Humankind*, by Yuval Noah Harari, the author talks about how Homo Sapiens are a social animal, and that social cooperation is actually the secret of our success as a species. So it's logical that we actually like people who help us or are friendly towards us.

Thirdly, we like people who are similar to ourselves because we can understand them. This again is part of the long history of Homo sapiens because we often function most effectively in small social groups, like families or tribes. In the past, people would rarely associate with others who were not like them unless forced to by work or circumstances. People are attracted to people who are like themselves, so finding common ground is often what we are looking for when meeting new people.

In Britain, the weather is the perfect tool to create common ground. How often have you found yourself starting a conversation with a stranger about the weather? You might then search for other clues like their accent and ask where they are from. Then you might try to find people in common, and fine-tune your search for areas of crossover. When you find someone who is a match for you in lots of areas, you rarely forget that person.

Remember My Name

So how can you use this in your business? Number one, remember people's names. Dale Carnegie said, "If you remember my name, you pay me a subtle compliment; you indicate that I have made an impression on you. Remember my name and you add to my feeling of importance."

If you remember my name, I know you cared enough to remember me which is a compliment, and we're predisposed to like compliments and the people who give them. Another compliment is remembering what I like, what I think, or what I said. It's the same behaviour we're working with, so remember that my favourite whisky is heavily peated the second time I walk into your shop and, you guessed it, I'm a fan.

Flattery

Outright compliments are also good, but it's best to stay away from personal compliments about bodies or other subjective areas. But complimenting their choice of shoes or a t-shirt print is passable.

When you have a team, complimenting them when they do something good is a great way of building rapport. Not only that, when you keep your staff happy, you keep your customers content. If your staff are not happy, this will come across to your customers. The welfare of your staff and their motivation is a key area that most businesses miss. By using likeability and reciprocity with your staff, you help keep your business running well. Try giving out unexpected holidays or event tickets to them and you'll usually find they are more committed to the cause than ever.

Summary

This chapter has shown you a few easy wins with some simple and intuitive tools you can bake into your business. Some are obvious, as we've been doing them naturally for years, whilst others may not be obvious until now. These tools are used on us every day, some with good reason and some with hidden agendas. It is up to you to use these tools for the benefit of your customers, as well as yourself. If you are caught being sneaky and disingenuous with your customers, you will likely lose that customer for good. So my mantra for this, and for most of what I do in business, is the golden rule that my mum always used to say to me…"treat others as you wish to be treated".

THIRTEEN

Creativity

In the next few chapters, we'll look at the skills an entrepreneur needs to build a business and survive the travails of commerce. This chapter is about being creative. If you don't think you're creative, I think you might be wrong.

There are 7.35 billion people in the world, each of whom has a brain that lets them be creative, from the child playing with sticks in rural Europe to the piano student in Japan, or the chef in a hot, busy diner in Florida. Everyone has creative ability, without exception. It is the creative process that has allowed human beings to be the most successful mammal on this planet.

So, if we're all creative, why have I heard this statement so many times before: "It's ok for you, but I don't have a creative bone in my body"? Well, the metaphorical "creative bone" is, in fact, more like a "creative muscle". Unlike bones, muscles grow through use.

Similarly, maybe it is the common understanding of what

"being creative" means that leads us to believe some have it and some don't. It's true that being a "creative" is a title usually attributed to painters, writers, photographers, playwrights, actors, and musicians. Most of these roles are in the "creative" fields or the Arts. Creativity is found in the essence of these roles, as well as in the function of them. However, that essence is also found in engineers, mathematicians, scientists, and middle managers. Managers might take a little more of a leap of faith to believe, but it is true, and I'll explain why.

How You Are Creative

The definition of Creativity is: the use of imagination or original ideas to create something. Creativity is not about what you *do*—it is about how you use your brain.

To understand this better, let's swap the term "creativity" for "problem-solving". In light of that simple change, it's probable that everyone can grasp the ability to be creative.

Designers solve the problem of making a page readable, useful, and attractive to communicate a message to you through text, pictures, colour, and space. This kind of problem-solving may not appear to be as crucial as engineers solving problems like carbon extraction from the atmosphere. However, it is no less a use of the creative problem-solving mind.

When I started the third job of my career, I was a graphic designer at a business which was very broad in their creative output. Some agencies stick to print or web, and those specialists have a place, but the agency I was at had graphic designers, 3D designers, product designers, and architectural designers. After a mind-expanding four years there, I realised that graphic design was only one part of design. In that time, I'd gone from being a heavily print-based designer to working on software interfaces, visitor attractions, big-brand retail experiences, exhibition stands, building visitor flows, product design, and interactive displays. I could see that once you allow the creative thought process to flow, all you need to do is add the parameters of the brief and start the brain thinking—all the brain was doing was solving a given problem.

The Creative Process

The process of creative problem-solving happens in many areas that are not obviously known for their creativity. For example, the small restaurant owner has to create a menu that will attract customers. They have to choose a decor that creates the right atmosphere for their style of food. Then they have to fine-tune the menu once customers start rolling in, noticing what sells and what doesn't. They may then need to adapt how the food arrives at the table—maybe there's one too many tables in the restaurant, which restricts service staff going in and out of the kitchen. Maybe the restaurant feels cramped—people need space, and this could have a long-term negative effect on repeat custom. None of this is seen as "creative" and in fact, the owner probably outsourced the so-called "creative" process of signage, promotional literature, and table menus to a designer. However, all of these issues require the power of a creative brain, and a problem-solving mind.

Let's look at it like this: what if there was an alternative multi-verse earth much like ours? Humans on that tiny identical earth didn't have the problem-solving abilities we have. How far do you think they would have got? They might have made fire, but it would have been purely by accident. They wouldn't have reached the use of early tools, nor the wheel, which means there would be no agriculture. And I'm pretty certain we'd all be eating foraged food. We'd grunt as there would likely be nothing like our language either. Communication would be a huge barrier that they probably wouldn't be able to solve.

Fortunately, we were blessed with a problem-solving ability that has helped us build shelter, grow food, and communicate with each other. Communication has enabled us to build shelters that reach the sky and create all sorts of technical and amazing things.

A Bit of Science

This is what actually happens when you are being creative. There was once a train of thought that the right-hand side of your brain was for logic and the left-hand side was for creative ideas. However, these days neuroscientists have discovered that it's not as simple as that. The creative process uses a number of parts of the brain, namely the Executive Attention Network, the Imagination Network, and the Salience Network. These areas work together to help us think of ideas, to imagine what would happen, even before we implement and simulate an idea and correct it for a different outcome—all within milliseconds.

Here it is in technical terms:

The brain uses the Executive Attention Network when a task requires focussed attention. This network is active when you are concentrating on something like a complex problem or listening to instructions. This puts heavy demands on your working memory. The neural architecture involved requires efficient and reliable communication between lateral (outer) regions of the prefrontal cortex and areas toward the back (posterior) of the parietal lobe.

The Default Network, or Imagination Network, is involved in constructing mental simulations, based on personal past experiences. This occurs when you are trying to remember something or thinking about the future, and when you imagine alternative scenarios. The Imagination Network is also involved in social cognition. It is active when imagining what a customer might be thinking. This area of the brain utilises areas deep inside the prefrontal cortex and temporal lobe (medial regions), and communication with various outer and inner regions of the parietal cortex.

The Salience Network constantly monitors external events and our internal stream of consciousness. It passes the information to the most important part of our brain to solve the task. This network consists of the dorsal anterior cingulate cortices and anterior insular and is important for dynamic switching between different areas of the brain.

(Extracted from a blog post by of Dr Scott Barry Kaufman)

What this means is—we all have the biological hardware in-built to be creative, in fact, it is what makes us human.

. . .

Summary

To sum it up, creativity is not the preserve of a few—it is the essence of being human. We are all creators, problem-solvers, and thinkers. Much like in the gym, some people have bigger muscles than others. Some people's muscles are maybe not as obvious as others, but they are just as strong. There is always room in this gym to train and build your creative muscle... the more you use it, the more it grows.

I challenge you to recalibrate your understanding of creativity and see yourself in the same light as some of the masters—Isambard Kingdom Brunel, Beethoven, Da Vinci, and Einstein. They are your peers. They may have more obvious creative muscles than you, but if you put the effort in, you could easily surpass your own expectations.

FOURTEEN

Problem-Solving

In the previous chapter, we looked at creativity and how we can substitute this word for "problem-solving". In this chapter, we'll look at problem-solving from a more practical standpoint.

Problem-solving is not unique to humans, and there are many animals who have the ability to work out problems. These animals tend to be the ones with a larger brain relative to their body size. We know that the octopus and the dolphin are very intelligent, but the bear is also great at problem-solving. However, if we look at the human species, this is one of our outstanding features: the ability to solve complex problems rather than simple ones. As we touched on at the end of the last chapter, this largely comes from our pre-frontal cortex. That is the front part of your brain, behind your forehead and temples. This area of the brain is wired to other networks or areas, which allows us to access memories, abstract thinking, sensory processing, performance, motor control, and emotions. All of which are necessary for problem-solving.

Understanding and solving complex problems is an everyday occurrence for us humans. Running your own business may require you to do a lot more problem-solving. As a business owner, you not only have the complexity of the service or skill you are selling, you also have to manage customers, accounts, and project cashflow, and manage all of these with no safety net or superiors to call on for help. In a career, you often train to be first class at one thing, such as management, accountancy, pharmacy, plumbing, or operating a CNC machine. However, as a business owner, you also have to do the things you are not first class at. For example, my skills are in design, but as a business owner, I also need to keep an eye on my accounts. Numbers are not in my natural skill set, so they're something I have to work hard at. For each type of business out there, the owner is taking on not only their best or key skill, but also their worst skill.

If you're stepping out on your own for the first time, you'll encounter many things that you have no idea how to do, and this may seem daunting. Don't let that stop you though, as there are always many ways to get something done.

Problem-Solution-Implementation.

Problem-Solution-Implementation (or P-S-I) looks like this:

- Problem: The key is to identify the problem in the first place.

- Solution: Then you must understand it fully and research solutions.
- Implementation: Then select the best possible solution and implement "the fix".

You may need to try a few solutions before you have the problem fully solved, but in my experience, this often falls into the Problem-Solution-Implementation-New Problem-New Solution-New Implementation process and goes round like this until the problem is fully solved.

So let's look at this in terms of the issues we'll encounter in a new business. As I mentioned earlier, in any new business, there will be dozens of issues you have never come across before. One of the easiest ways to solve these problems is to outsource them or bring in other people who do have those skills.

In the P-S-I methodology, this can be identified as Problem (bookkeeping) — Solution (identify local bookkeepers, get recommendations from other business owners) — Implementation (call two of the best bookkeepers and interview them, then select the one you want to work with).

The best kind of problem-solving is probably outsourcing your problems to someone else, as this allows you to focus on the things you are good at.

However, sometimes this can't be done for various reasons. It may be that you started the business and it's just you. The issue might be that you need to perform a sales pitch. The P-S-I for this is: identify the problem, which might be your public speaking confidence. Find a solution by searching for public speaking courses, or find someone to help you with that aspect of your confidence. If the issue is more about the content of the pitch, search online for "how to construct a pitch". The P-S-I methodology even works as a pitching outline itself. What is the problem you see? What is the solution you provide? How will you implement the solution?

P-S-I helps with most issues in business—even the really boring tasks like finding couriers, waste disposal, grounds maintenance, cleaners, and PAT testing. Even health and safety risk assessments are P-S-I based.

For me, P-S-I became very clear when I worked in the design agency I previously mentioned. We would often discuss new projects at a meeting table in the studio. Before long, the ideas started flowing and each one built on the back of the last until we finished the meeting with a framework of what we wanted to create. The P-S-I model here was most often P-S-P-S-P-S, because we would solve the problem only for the solution to create a new problem or a new angle of the problem. We wouldn't stop the meeting until we had settled on the best solution, and only then did we go away to implement it.

It reminded me of art lessons at school. As a design team, it's like we were all sculptors, seated around the table with this great chunk of clay (the idea) sat in front of us. As someone offered an idea, a piece of clay would be trimmed off. Then someone else would throw in another idea, which would remove more bits of clay. Then a "You can't do that because of this" comment, and a bit of clay would be stuck back onto the block. But before long, this exchange of ideas, or problems and solutions, would turn this lump of clay into a stunning piece of art ready for the furnace, to be fired and turned into something solid.

Urgent Important

Your business or service will undoubtedly have a myriad of problems, some great, some tiny. Which ones you pick first will depend on you. You can start at the easy end, giving yourself momentum, or go for the big ones that take a while, but make all the other problems disappear once they've been cracked. I often go for a mid-size issue first, as the small ones often feel like moving a pile of sand with a thimble and the large ones feel immovable like a heavy boulder.

I also use a tool for this, which you can find anywhere online by searching for "Urgent Important Matrix". This matrix has four boxes, two on top of another two. The matrix reads, Urgent - Not Urgent across the top and Important - Not Important down the side. You then place the job/issue in whichever box you determine it to be. If it's either Urgent - Important or Not Urgent – Important, these are the jobs you should put the most effort into. Then Urgent - Not Important and Not Urgent - Not Important.

A Scenario

As an example of problem-solving, let's imagine you are in a product business, like a toy shop. You may have a money problem, which first appears like you have a bad business, the consequences being you will go bust in a month or two. That is a considerable problem.

Problem: Lack of income.

Solution: Get some money.

On deeper inspection, we break it down and find that the problem is actually that you don't have enough money because you don't have enough sales. And that's because you don't have enough customers.

Looking deeper still, you might find the problem is that no one knows the shop exists. The real problem is you don't have enough customers because the shop is in a back alley, away from the main shopping areas, and the shop is in disrepair.

Now we have a more tangible problem to deal with than "we don't have enough income".

Problem: Low footfall because shop is in a backstreet.

Solution: Move the shop or improve footfall.

Implementation: We can't afford to move the shop, but let's get a couple of A-boards that we can stick at the end of the street with directional arrows pointing to the shop.

Problem: Unwelcoming shop front.

Solution: Fix it up, clean the windows, paint the frontage, and get some new signs done.

Implementation: Buy the paint and order the signs.

Problem: No one knows about the shop.

Solution: Inform local stores down the street to the main shopping areas that you are there.

Implementation: Drop off flyers and even cakes or gifts to the owners, who may give you referrals. Then do something that gets you noticed. For example, hire a costumed salesperson or hand out leaflets to people yourself. Create a mini-stall where you can stand and sell the goods. You'll have limited stock available, but you can say "I can have it here in a minute from my store, which by the way has many more items". This prompts them to think about visiting the store themselves to see what you have.

Problem: No one knows about the shop.

Solution: Get in the local press

Implementation: Do a piece in local publications. If it's a toy shop, donate some toys to a playgroup.

Problem: Price-driven customers, no loyalty.

Solution: Target a small group of people who will become loyal fans.

Implementation: When a customer turns up at the shop,

take VIP care of them. Offer them refreshments, show them around and explain the ranges, what's new in, and so on. Then if they leave without a purchase, take their details to enter them into a big prize draw. Give them a postcard for them to remember you by. If they do purchase something, wrap it up really neatly, but do ask them as they may be in a hurry. Then offer them a discount voucher for their next sale, "In fact, have two, maybe you have a friend..." You may lose a little margin, but creating loyal customers has long-term benefits.

Problem: Not enough income.

Solution: Get customers to know about you.

Implementation: Advertise your shop through word of mouth by making happy customers.

If you make your customers' lives easier and more fulfilling, then you will gain loyal fans.

Summary

Every business owner knows their own problems, but asking deeper questions about that problem can reframe the solution. It's like noticing that the bath isn't filling up and just turning the tap on more without realising the problem is that there's no plug. Isolating the problem and breaking bigger problems down into smaller sub-problems gives you the ability to create solutions that are actually effective. You then have a real chance of getting somewhere.

To recap, we're problem-solving animals. Outsource what problems you can. Use the P-S-I method to fix big or small issues. Finally, break problems down into smaller sub-problems.

FIFTEEN

Less Is More

Once you have started on the entrepreneurial journey, you'll find that things quickly begin to get away from you. You have a great idea, and it spawns a boat-load of effort to take it forward, but the uphill struggle is offset by the fun of doing something new. Before long, you have a list of responsibilities as long as your arm, with multiple clients or customers demanding your attention. Then, the joy of creating something exciting can turn into a chore.

This happened in my business around year three. In that time, we'd seen our turnover double every year, then external issues in the wider economy hit us hard. The excitement of growth began to slow down, and the fun was gone. We'd experienced many exciting things during that time—people approaching us about a possible acquisition, and being featured in dozens of magazines and websites, even several TV shows. Like an addict, I wanted to feel that same rush I got when I started the company. So I got side-tracked into more and more side projects.

In hindsight, I see that I was side-tracked, but at the time, I thought these projects were legitimate business opportunities. Each of them had their brief sparkle in the sky, before fading. On the plus side, many of those projects enabled me to write this book. However, at the time I got so good at creating and designing products and brands that I forgot about the utility or viability of the product. I focussed solely on the fun part of creating something, building websites, printing brochures, and doing social media and PR.

I think a defining lesson here is that maybe you need to limit the financial and time exposure of a legitimate opportunity until it is clear you have a viable opportunity.

At one point in time I had about six or seven products, all of which had their own brand, website, and social channels. They were all running from the same building with the same team, who I expected to be as enthused about each new idea as I was. Then another external issue raised its ugly head— Google changing its algorithm and wiping out our online revenue almost overnight. Our online sales were what paid the staff wages every month. So when sales dropped significantly, "we" became "me".

Simplicity

Out of necessity, I closed down five of the products as I couldn't do all the work on my own. But out of this bad situation, I learned a great lesson. That is, less is more.

Less time managing brand profiles meant more time making two of the brands better, so that's what I did. The entrepreneurial journey is a mix of highs and lows. Usually, more highs than lows, but 96% of businesses fail in the first ten years. This is probably because one of those lows just didn't seem worth coming back from.

For me, it *was* worth it, because within 18 months I was having my best year. Less time divided by many types of customers meant more time to make the few happier. Less money spent on marketing multiple brands meant more resources to create a better product in the areas we were still in.

Do One Thing Well

If you are only at the beginning of your journey, this might not crop up for a while, but be aware of the trap you may set yourself. If you remain focussed on the vision or the dream, then you'll be able to stay on track. But the lesson is almost simpler than that—contrary to the "don't put all your eggs in one basket" concept—put of all your effort into that one thing. With that effort, you'll see big gains. Live and breathe your business and it will take on a life of its own. Passion is infectious, so when you love your thing, people want to do business with you.

If you find yourself tiring of where you are in a couple of years' time, sit back and take stock. Look objectively at the business and ask yourself: is it actually working, are people using your services, or is your dissatisfaction a symptom of a deeper problem? If the business is healthy, and it is *you* who have lost your way, find and create a new role for yourself in your own company to try bring back some passion. I have done this on a few occasions. Yes I still have to look after many areas, but when I reframe my role as the Growth Hacker or the Quality Control person I find a new lease of life.

If the business isn't healthy and that is what is tiring you, find the weaknesses and work on those. For instance, if sales are poor, focus as much on marketing as possible, even getting help. If it is the lack of quality and/or you get negative feedback about your products, focus on fixing those issues. Put your energy into the one thing that needs the change.

Look at the existing business, rather than looking outside, and push again. Sometimes just shifting the furniture around in your place of work is enough to pick you up. If that's too low-level for you, speak to your customers, the ones you like. Get their feedback on what you do. If they say that your product or service is vital to them, your spirits should lift, because your little thing is crucial to someone else.

In business, we try to hire the best person for the skill set we need. If that is marketing, you probably won't hire a bricklayer who does a bit of marketing on the side. This isn't because bricklayers can't be good marketers—they can. But it's that we'd expect someone who is good at marketing to be doing it full time. If they aren't, we can legitimately question how good they actually are. The same goes for your customers.

Spread yourself too thin and customers may worry that you aren't good enough at "the one thing". This is why I always hesitate to link my two main brands, because to customers they are very different. In my world, they use the same machinery and skills, but to the customer, they are in different sectors and appear to be unrelated. This can be a little mind speed bump in the way of a smooth sale. So I generally market these two areas completely separately. Because less is more in your customers' eyes too.

Summary

Remember the advice from the company ethos chapter: *What do you want to be known for?* If you pick too many things to be known for, you will tie yourself up in knots trying to stick to the company values to the detriment of your productivity. The same applies here. Just be great at that one thing you have passion for and people will get to know what you're about. Deep is often better than wide in this sense.

I often recall or remember this saying: "Good is the enemy of great". Diverting your resources to other projects is good, but staying the course and keeping your focus is great.

SIXTEEN

Carpe Momentum

AKA "GET ON A PLANE"

Carpe Diem is Latin for "seize the day", and *Carpe Momentum* means "seize the moment". That is what this chapter is all about. It's a balance of your ambition and your regret. You can either seize the moment or regret it passing.

As we near the end of the book I want to impress on you that this chapter is a fundamental lesson that could simply read "nothing happens without effort". I could end this chapter right there, but instead, I'll tell you the lessons I learned through my trials and failure, so that you don't have to make the same mistakes. Or at least when opportunity offers you something, you can recognise it and grab it with both hands.

I have a mantra I now like to remind myself of: "Get on a plane". This mantra came from a couple of episodes in my life where I realised that my hesitation cost me an opportunity. The foundation of this way of thinking came from my experiences with two overseas clients. Over time, it became obvious that almost all opportunities are a balance of risk and reward. "Get on a plane" could as easily have been, "Get on a train", "Get in the car" or even "Get on the phone".

Lesson #1 - Going the Extra Mile

Back in 2009, I had a website selling gadget skins, which were printed stickers that wrapped the back of a phone, tablet, or laptop. One day, I was asked whether I would create some wraps for a Finnish games company. At the time, the company's name wasn't in the public eye, but they were behind one of the world's biggest iPhone games. Like many other people, I had the game on my phone. The game was a phenomenal success; however, it sort of overshadowed the company.

The company wanted to brand all their team devices with the company name and logo which was all I was asked for. But rather than just settle for the corporate team branded skins, I tried to create an opportunity to produce these skins for retail with the game graphics. To do this, I created a memorable packaging solution, getting my dad to build a large bird box to ship the stickers in. I created a few retail-style sample versions of skins on iPad and iPhone and included them in with the corporate skins we shipped. Thankfully, they were a hit, and we were asked whether we would be interested in putting some ideas and costs together for supplying the game branded skins for retail outlets. Mission accomplished, or so I thought. However, that was the easy bit, now came the tricky bit.

I heavily rely on my creative brain and try to leave the

other stuff to someone else, so I asked a good friend to go through the numbers with me. These were big numbers. The potential upside was huge, because news had come out that they were selling a million game-inspired soft toys per month.

After submitting the costs to the team, I waited and waited, not something I'm good at. After a few weeks, I sent a few more emails to which the reply was that the proposal had been sent to the licensing division to get approval.

I eventually got an email from the licensing division asking how I would like to proceed: as a supplier or to purchase the licence.

A supplier would make the product and then sell it to the brand owner for them to arrange reselling in retail stores. Whereas a licence holder, buys the rights to manufacture the product and then they arrange for the product to be sold in retail stores.

So when I asked to be a supplier rather than buy the licence, it was the end of the road. Why? In hindsight, I should have bought the licence. When dealing with a fast-moving company, who are more used to building games than retail opportunities, to opt for purchasing the licence would have been the better option.

I may be simplifying the process because either way it would have meant a significant investment in staff and machinery. However, as an aside, it does show just how easy it is to reach out and grab a multimillion-pound deal if we only put the effort in. There is always a trade-off of risk and reward for every significant opportunity.

So what has the "Get on the plane" bit got to do with this story I hear you say?

What could I have done to improve my odds? I should have bought a ticket to Finland and door-stepped the Licensing Department, then taken them out for coffee or bought them some cream cakes. This is a tool to become memorable—when we meet in person, it is harder for people to dismiss us. If you create rapport and discuss things outside the deal, such as family life, you become a real person with hopes and dreams. Your face becomes logged in the other person's mind, then when your email pops up again, they are more likely to remember you and favour you.

The next story is not dissimilar. I want to impress on you how much "getting out your own way" is crucial to doing great things.

Lesson #2 - Grab the Opportunity

Not far away from where my studio is based, there is a company called Twisted who specialise in Land Rover Defender vehicles. They were sponsoring the Gumball 3000 road rally, which is a trip across a continent or two, in luxury vehicles like a Ferraris or Lamborghinis. As a sponsor, Twisted had a few vehicles on the trip, one of which was being used by Tony Hawk, the pro-skater and another by MTV.

For me, the story started when the company posted a picture of a white Land Rover on their Instagram with "Proud to have Tony Hawk driving our vehicle". I screen-grabbed the image, photoshopped some funky vehicle-wrapping graphics on to it, and posted it back to them within a few minutes.

Over the coming weeks, I built up the relationship and eventually I got in my plane, sorry, car, and drove to see them. Success! Because I did this I was paid to design and wrap three of the four Twisted vehicles for Gumball. I wrapped the Land Rover that Tony Hawk used, which I was a little bit excited about.

Lesson #3 – Meet In Person

The saying "It is not what you know, but who you know" is truer than ever. In the world of social media, you may appear to know everything there is to know, but the person who gets out there and speaks to people is the person who will walk away with the deal.

In person, we weigh each other up, smile, mirror each other's body language, and get a sense of whether we want to do business with the person. With all of those psychological and physiological signals going on, there is one key benefit that a "personal meet-up" can have over a digital one. It is called "the mere exposure effect" (also known as the familiarity principle). It suggests that simply being repeatedly exposed to a person, thing, or idea increases our liking of it. The more time you spend with someone, the more likely you are to have a preference and positive opinion of them.

Following on from the last story, after we had posted pictures of our Twisted vehicle wraps, another Gumball team started chatting with us—Team68. We developed a great rapport with Team68 and over time, we had the opportunity to design for them. We also offered some design ideas to one of their friends who makes luxury powerboats.

This boat brand was lucky enough to lead out the super-exclusive Venture Cup, an offshore powerboat race. AJ and Håvard, who were working with the company, attended the Boat Show in London, and it just happened that I was working on the outskirts of London at the time. We arranged to meet at the Boat Show and maybe have a few drinks afterwards.

However, I started to think negatively. I'd had a long day and felt drained, having worked longer than expected the night before and that day. I started coming up with excuses like "The show would be closing as I got there" and "The M25 motorway is a nightmare…especially around rush-hour!" and "The hotels will be expensive near the Boat Show". So I bailed out. I let momentary feelings get in the way of a personal meet and greet. I actually missed the opportunity to put a personal face to the ideas we had been discussing and lost the opportunity to press forward and become an official designer on the project.

Failing to meet Team68 in person didn't just happen once —it happened twice. The second time, I was invited over to Norway, the land of the midnight sun, for a boat race as a guest. I looked at my workload, the cost of flights, my cash flow at that time, and then my excuses kicked in and I bottled it. Again.

You have to get on the plane, or the train, or the boat, or in your car. You never know where things might take you, but you will always regret not going for it. I'm not a shrinking violet by any means, but sometimes I really have to push myself out of my comfort zone. I'm in my safe place behind the screen of my computer, which is where I've spent the best part of my professional career. Sadly for me, the real deals get done in person.

Going back over my own errors, I should have got on the plane to see Team68, because who knows where it could have led? I should have bought a ticket to Finland and taken the game company's licensing team for a coffee. I should have pushed myself out of my own comfort zone. When I have done this, good things have happened and when I haven't, all I've been left with is regret.

Just to add a more positive note to this, I did actually meet Team68 in person and I now work closely with them on projects.

So "get on your metaphorical plane" and make things happen.

SEVENTEEN

Dreaming Bigger

This last chapter is like the team talk before you meet your challengers. If it serves you, imagine me on a soap-box, or better still, imagine [insert your favourite speaker or team coach] talking you through this next chapter in an excited manner.

I often say "stop dreaming and start doing". That's because I'm passionate about the "doing" bit. I'm no business god. Like most people, some days I procrastinate. Especially before doing tasks outside my comfort zone. I'm quite happy flipping between the thinking tasks and the making, or physical tasks, using my head and my hands.

This is where you come in. You see, I might have a certain ability or skill, but I know I'm not good at many other things—and that's why I have a team of people who get stuff done with me, some as my team, some as sub-contractors, others as suppliers. I'm not a good bookkeeper, so I have someone for that. I'm not a good web designer, so I have someone else for that. All of us are different, with huge skill differences and abilities. We also have vastly different likes and dislikes. Couple that with the fact that we all have different homes, lives, and money needs. As such, it's obvious to me that one book will never cover the right amount of content for you specifically. So as part of this journey, you need to read a lot more because the world needs your ideas, your skills, "your take on things", and it needs you to step up and go for it!

Must Do Better

When I was a kid, more than one of my school reports said: "would do better if he didn't spend his time looking out of the window dreaming". I even got moved to another desk in French lessons for exactly that reason. I am a dreamer. For me, there is no limit to what can be achieved by humans, except maybe to save themselves from themselves, but we'll leave politics for another book.

The reason I know that we can do anything we put our mind to is because of how I learned an instrument. I never did music at school, and my parents never even thought about me being musical, but at 21 I picked up a guitar and decided I wanted to learn. Like everyone, I was rubbish at first, but I played and played, every single day, for ten minutes or two hours. Within a year, I was playing my guitar in front of small audiences, and shortly after that, large audiences of up to 400 people. I'm no John Squire, but I can play. If I can do that just because I decided to do it, I know that if you *really* want to start your own business, then you can.

· · ·

Exciting Times

Now you have your idea, what do you do with it? You live in the best time, ever! There couldn't be more opportunity sat there waiting for you. There are resources that couldn't even be dreamed of ten years ago. You can listen to the world's best in your area of interest on podcasts and YouTube videos. You couldn't actually read all of the information that is out there, on even the tiniest of niches!

If by some miracle, you've found a niche that doesn't have lots of content, then it's something that should be exploited —not an excuse to do nothing. Get out and write about it, make it known, and crown yourself the king or queen of the world's most obscure niche.

If your area already has lots of content, you might feel you are giving yourself a hard time because everyone is in that space already. But tell yourself this—if everyone is in that space, it must be worth it! So dive in and make a name for yourself as the newbie on the block looking to take the crown.

If your area is oversaturated and there's no way of making yet another million-hit YouTube channel or a zillion-follower Snapchat in this field, don't worry. Start with a manageable goal—all you need is 10 fans. When you hit that, aim for 100, then when you hit that, aim for 250, 500, and 1000. At your 1000 fans party that you have with your cat, launch the 3000 fan goal. Say you don't make it to 3000, and stall at 2811 fans—well, that's more than you had at the start. As much as I love Tim Ferriss, Gary Vaynerchuk, Richard Branson, and Elon Musk, we don't need another one. So stop worrying about being one of them!

Just Get Going

There are lots of reasons not to start your dream business, it is easy to procrastinate because of fear. It would be fair to say that if you have a partner and children that depend on you, there is risk. Fear of the risks you are taking are real and should be considered. But even then, you should recognise those fears and still make a plan and position yourself to make the step in two or six months, a year at the longest. You'll never know enough about your area to start, so you just need to start. You probably will never have enough money saved to cover all the issues you will have in the next year. No book, course, or even coaching will prepare you for the rubber hitting the road, so don't let any of that be your stopping point. If this really is your dream, you need to start doing something—it will not just come to you.

When you have made the big leap, you're making it happen, and things are going in the right direction, then you need to start dreaming bigger. *What?* I hear you say. *You just told me to stop dreaming, now you're telling me to dream?*

Yes, just like that kid in French class, I needed to pay attention to where I was at that time. But once you've made the move, it's time to keep your head above the tide and start dreaming big. Work in your business will swallow you up if you're not careful, so you need to stay above it all. Keeping your dream in your mind will help you do that.

When you close in on that dream, build a bigger and more expansive dream! It doesn't have to be all about you either —as you build a team of people and a network, you can have a dream for your people too. When you have people, you will need to lead and pass on the dream. Keeping your head above the work or operational activities at least once a week will help you to stay on track. I have a notepad I write in regularly that contains the vision for my business. I also have a coach who helps me think beyond the minutia of daily tasks. And I keep in regular contact with other business owners and talk about goals and dreams.

Standing on the Shoulders of Giants

Facebook and Google are exceptional companies, so using them as a benchmark for comparison is a little naughty of me. However, these companies started out with one action. They started out with one dream and gradually built up to what they are today, monoliths of the internet era. Both of these companies are your springboard! If they could build such mammoth businesses with global reach, imagine what you can do standing on their shoulders!

For most of my working life, I've been involved with the internet of some sort. With the old dial-up modems, dialling in for customer emails and downloading files. Now you can have files of 1GB downloading at lightening speeds. We have cloud computing, meaning we can process complex tasks on someone else's computer, save files to them, and have everything sync on all of our devices. More robots and AI are coming online every day, and whilst we could be scared of that kind of tech, imagine a world where we have built structures and conventions that keep us safe. Imagine what AI could do in working out the DNA of many problems related to our health and ageing. Or it could be used to find new, sustainable ways to make products. Robots of all sorts, "humanoid" or "car factory-style", could make the riskiest jobs something that humans no longer have to do. Maybe I'm going a bit too far into the future, but the point is to dream at a level that spurs you to achieve great things.

Step up and Go

Bringing us back to reality, nothing happens unless you *actually do something*. Unless you make a move, quit the job, or start the evening work, nothing changes. You are no closer to the dream, so it will end up as just that—a dream, which is a series of thoughts, images, and sensations occurring in a person's mind.

When you're old, are you going to regret not going for it while you could? Or going for it and not making it? Which is worse? It turns out that nearly all regrets are based on "not knowing". By all means, be sensible—betting it all on red might not be the smartest idea. But if you build your dream gradually and iron out the kinks of your idea, that dream will become a reality.

Monday Mornings

One final note I think is motivation enough to get started. I remember those weekends that went too fast, Monday morning seemed to loom on Friday even before I left work. These days, I look forward to going into work. I come back from holiday happy and ready for work. Whilst some people love their job that much, not many people can say that outside of being a small business owner.

You have the world at your fingertips. At the end of that internet cable is all the resources you need from teaching and training, coaching, and peer groups. There are printers and factories ready to create your idea. There are people in need of your skills, right here in your town, but also at the other side of the world. The financial resources needed to trade internationally are so low they're not worth considering, especially when you compare it to even fifteen, maybe even ten years ago.

The world—once connected by trade routes and shipping lanes—became connected by telegraph wires and later telecom wires. Now, the world is connected by satellites in space and noughts and ones. The digital era has levelled the playing field for almost all industries, and few major industries have yet to come under the pressure of this new democratised world.

There Are No More Excuses

As I've said before, I'm all for a bit of dreaming—it's fundamental to find your north star, but don't be a stargazer. Get up, roll up your sleeves, and start creating something. For the vast majority of people, the worst thing that can happen is you lose a bit of money and learn some lessons.

When you've built that business, that lifestyle you want, then stop doing and start dreaming of your next adventure. Doing so is a process, and like riding a bike (if you like riding bikes down rocky trails), it can be great fun and a rush, if a little scary at times. But facing your fears is actually what gives you that satisfaction in life. If you can say that you dreamt up a business, you created it, you built it, and nurtured it into a fully functional business, then you have slain the big hairy beast of regret sitting at the end of your bed in many years' time.

So what are you waiting for?

Outro

Oh my goodness, I cannot believe I actually did that. I actually wrote a book!

As a poor academic student, (I got an E for English, which explains a lot), I'm sure you can understand my relief at finishing this. I just want to thank you for sticking with it and getting to this point.

As I've pointed out a few times, I'm only a man and sub-par in many ways—I am no business god. I've not made millions, yet. I'm not on any top ten success list, and I can't even be on a "40 under 40" list anymore. All I'm good at is starting things. I'm a dreamer and a doer. My dreams could be bigger and maybe my "doing" needs to be greater, but the purpose of this book is to show you what you, or anyone, can do. Because if an ordinary someone like me can do it, you can too!

This book should only be seen as a first step on a ladder—you'll need to read and learn more, but most importantly, you just need to get started. Reading is no substitute for doing it, and reading is not a ladder that starts halfway up the wall of success, but it does help. So keep reading and climbing.

So here we are, at the end of the book, and if you made it this far, I think you deserve a medal. I hope you've gained some insights and practical tips that will help you start your dream business. With the sidepreneur movement in full swing, you don't even need to quit your job to start something today.

The reality is, and I don't use this sentence lightly, there has never been a better time to start something!

Thank You

I couldn't have written this book without all of these people.

Firstly, to my long-suffering wife Nicola, who puts up with me, especially my dreaming, my highs and lows, and the long hours and absence whilst pursuing business goals. My kids, who are the reason I push myself—I thrive on the love they give.

I want to thank my parents. I wouldn't be the guy I am today without my inspirational and creative dad, who I am proud of. To my mum, who is one of the most beautiful souls you could ever meet. Love you mum. My little sis Chrissie, who cares about everyone, above and beyond. My brother Dan, who is way more of a people-person than I am and pushes me to become more all the time without knowing it. Martin, thanks for the helping me edit this book.

To my wider family and my proud Scottish heritage, even if we are all displaced far across the globe.

Then to my friends, pals, mates, buddies, crew, and gang, people I hope will buy my book, so I put their names in here: Jamie P, Fog, Ian, Clarky, Wayne, Sal, Ellen, Beth, Mr Windsor, Mark P, Nathan, Jason, Elis, Sam, and Mark Y.

People who inadvertently mentored or coached me. My Art & Business Studies teachers Mrs Cowdy and Mrs Knifton who started me on this journey unknowingly. Arris boys; Ian and Stuart. Gary S, Martin and David. Raymond, Guy, Dom, Dave K, Colin H, Marianne, Anton, and Ben.

My team throughout the years. Ben, Billy, Matt B, Stuart, Zak C, Zak B, Enzo, Nick, Jaz, Matt S, and Becky—thanks to you all for being part of building something.

Special mentions to:

Ed - You're the man. Miss working with you.

Jen - You are my favourite illustrator ever.

Tim - We nearly hit the big time.

Jamie F - True grafter. Solid-gold, five star.

The wider Dogtooth family, Dan, Sam, Alice, James, Lee, and all the many freelancers who helped me.

To the KPI17 crew Nicky, Paul, Jonas, Ben, Richard, George, Lee, Phil, Cody, Denise, Kavita, and Andrew. All the best on the journey—you guys rock. And to the Dent team—Daniel, you've built something that will have a big impact and will leave you a great legacy.

My old colleagues Nick, Jamie, Steve, Alison, Keith, and Rich.

Some people will never know they got thanked here. And some people who should have been thanked will have been missed. So if you're one of those people, I'm sorry, I'm a scatterbrain! But I am grateful for everyone and everything that made me who I am today.

Also by Rick Jesse

If you would like to read more along similar lines check out my
personal blog.

www.super808.com

If you want to check out my business head to our main website
where you can find links to the brands and products we manage
and produce.

www.dogtooth.co.uk

If you would like to contact me via email it is;

rick@designedtostick.co.uk

And you can follow me on Twitter @rickjesse

Printed in Great Britain
by Amazon